THE DAY TRADER'S COURSE WORKBOOK

T0334154

WILEY TRADING ADVANTAGE

THE DAY TRADER'S COURSE WORKBOOK

Step-by-Step Exercises to Help You Master The Day Trader's Course

Lewis Borsellino
with
Patricia Crisafulli

JOHN WILEY & SONS, INC.
New York • Chichester • Weinheim • Brisbane • Singapore • Toronto

Published by John Wiley & Sons, Inc.
Published simultaneously in Canada.

This publication is designed to provide accurate and authoritative information in regard to the subject matter covered. It is sold with the understanding that the publisher is not engaged in rendering legal, accounting, or other professional services. If legal advice or other expert assistance is required, the services of a competent professional person should be sought.

Designations used by companies to distinguish their products are often claimed as trademarks. In all instances where John Wiley & Sons, Inc. is aware of a claim, the product names appear in initial capital or all capital letters. Readers, however, should contact the appropriate companies for more complete information regarding trademarks and registration.

Library of Congress Cataloging in Publication Data:

Borsellino, Lewis J., 1957–
    The day trader's course workbook / Lewis Borsellino with Patricia Crisafulli.
       p.   cm.—(Wiley trading)
       ISBN 0-471-06517-X
       1. Day trading (Securities).   2. Electronic trading of securities
I. Crisafulli, Patricia. II. Title. III. Series.
   HG4515.95 .B673   2001
   332.64'2'0285—dc21   2001045304

10 9 8 7 6 5 4 3 2 1

Introduction

Writing *The Day Trader's Course* and the accompanying *Day Trader's Course Workbook* has been an interesting project, not only for me, but for the traders and technicians with whom I work every day.

This book and project have required us to break down, into specific steps and processes, things that—for me, after 20 years of trading—have become second nature.

It's far more than just "the market was going up" or "the market was going down." For every trader, there are (or at least there should be) a host of criteria that go into every trade. At any given time, any trader should be able to go through a log of a trade and ask, "Why did I make that trade?" Most importantly, ask yourself that question as you examine both the winners and the losers.

For all of us, the process of trading begins, continues, and ends with the chart. Where has the market been? Where is it likely to go? What are the key price levels—support, resistance, retracements, trend lines—up ahead? I call this the "ready" phase (as in "ready, aim, fire").

But "ready" begins before the market is open; it begins with reviewing what the market did the day before, and what we see as significant price levels on the radar screen. For so many traders—both beginners and those who are experienced—the transition from the premarket analysis to being in the thick of things is a challenging one.

At "aim," the market is live. What makes a marketplace is the confluence not only of buyers and sellers but also of various opinions and motivations. You may be a buyer at 1245, which means someone else is a seller at that level. Maybe you're initiating a long position in anticipation of the continuation of an uptrend, while someone else is either getting short in expectation of a reversal or exiting a long position established at a lower price.

During the trading day, we watch the market develop, mindful of our price targets, and navigate based on the charts, the volume, the momentum, and sometimes the general "noise" of the pit.

"Fire" is when it all comes together: the execution of the trade that you've been planning according to your strategy. But you don't fire randomly or at just any target. You've aimed with care, and you know where you'll get out for a profit or exit for a loss.

Of course, when you "fire," there is the question of how much. Are you trading small size—tentatively, in a market that may be very volatile or choppy? Or are you trading with size, for a position day trade because that matches your conviction but never exceeds your risk tolerance?

And then, of course, there is the element of surprise. On a given trading day, you might have to deal with an unexpected earnings warning from a leading technology company that causes the market to crater, or a surprise rate cut by the Federal Reserve (we saw a few of those in 2001) that causes a big spike up in the market.

That's the problem—and opportunity—of surprise. You may find yourself just as easily on the wrong side as the right one due to unforeseen circumstances. The only remedy is to trade each time with as much deliberate action and discipline as possible.

Always use a stop order to exit a losing trade. Never expose too much capital per trade. And always know why you make the trade.

In this *Workbook*, we have put together a review of the mental and technical sides of trading. For the beginning trader, I believe this *Workbook* and *The Day Trader's Course* it accompanies will serve as a good, solid introduction to the market and trading with a plan.

For those who already have been trading, this will serve as a refresher in some areas and remediation in others.

Remember, no matter how long you've been trading—or how long you *will* trade—you can never stop learning. And always, always pay attention to the lessons that the market is teaching you.

—LEWIS BORSELLINO
TeachTrade.com

Contents

QUESTIONS
AND EXERCISES

1
The Mental Game

Successful trading is 90 percent emotional and psychological and 10 percent technical. That's not to underestimate, by any means, the need to study and analyze the market. But the best trading system—the best signals and indicators—will be severely undermined if the mental side of your trading game is at all compromised.

Too many times traders look for a 100 percent accurate, never-fail trading system that will work in all markets, all the time. Based on my 20 years of trading, there is no surefire system or indicator. But I do know that there is one essential, regardless of your time frame, parameters, trading style, or experience level: discipline.

Without discipline, it becomes extremely difficult—if not impossible—for a trader to be successful.

The key to having discipline is to know yourself. You must be honest with yourself with regard to your risk tolerance and your ability—mentally—to handle the stresses of trading, in particular handling losses and handling winners.

Losses are inevitable in trading. No trading system—no trader, for that matter—is right every time. Too many "newbies" enter trading with a skewed vision of what it will be like. Their expectations are high for dollar performance. Remember, the first year of trading you shouldn't plan on making any money, other than to cover your commissions and other costs. If that's your expectation, you will not put pressure on yourself to trade excessively. Rather, your goal should be to gain experience and confidence in trading. This includes both technical analysis and trade execution.

Trading is a hands-on learning experience. All the books, videos, courses, and seminars won't replace the day in, day out experience of trading. A vital component of that experience is your own mental and emotional reaction to losses. By the same token, you must keep a level head when it comes to your wins. Over the years I've seen so many young traders blow it because they become overconfident. They have a week of wins—no down days at all. What happens then? They become convinced that they are invincible, that they have beaten the market. They take on too much risk, trade too big for their capital, and become sloppy in their discipline. You can guess what happens next . . . a big loss or string of losses that takes a large bite out of their capital, and potentially takes them out of the game.

YOUR TRADING PSYCHOLOGY

When it comes to the "mental game" of trading, it's important to forget about the market for a moment, and look inward. There is no one who can tell you about you—except you. Trading is not for everyone. I have known some very intelligent, highly successful individuals over the years who have distinguished themselves in their careers and reaped the financial rewards of their successes. But when it came to trading . . . well, that was another story.

Here's a psychological profile to get you thinking about your own personality, risk tolerance, and lifestyle. This may help you assess whether you really have the temperament to be a day trader or you're better suited to being an investor. Knowing your inherent style can help you make the best choices for yourself in the market. If you can't stomach risk, if you can't cut losses quickly and move on, then day trading may not be your best choice. Rather, if you enjoy the plotting out of a strategy and have the patience to stick with a position—and the discipline not to change or alter stops that limit your losses—you may find that you're an investor at heart.

(*Note:* This psychological profile is meant to be used only as a guide to help you assess your risk tolerance and your attraction to trading. Your score is in no way a guarantee of success or failure.)

Exercise 1.1

For each question, select the reply that best answers the question *for you*. Write the number of the response in the space provided.

1. Never applies to me.

2. Rarely applies to me.

3. Sometimes applies to me.

4. Often applies to me.

5. Definitely applies to me.

A. Markets have a mind of their own. They always   _____
    give me problems.

B. When it comes to trading, average-sized profits   _____
    will not be satisfying to me.

C. Developing a daily strategy based on market   _____
    analysis *is not* needed in order to succeed.

D. People think I'm a success when I trade large   _____
    quantities.

E. Being disciplined in trading *does not* increase my   _____
    chances to make consistent money.

F. I view the markets as presenting a 50–50 chance   _____
    of winning on every trade.

G. I believe the longer a market trend lasts, the better the chance it will continue.   _____

H. I want to be a trader because of the excitement.   _____

I. I view the market as one giant game in which I participate.   _____

J. I am in the market to be proven correct.   _____

K. I am in the market to make money.   _____

L. I want to be a trader because it's a neat lifestyle.   _____

M. I am patient enough to wait for my analysis to work, even if it means holding on to a trade for two weeks.   _____

N. I feel most comfortable exploiting short-term market swings during each trading day.   _____

O. Trading is great because you don't have to work very hard to be successful.   _____

P. I like to use my gut instinct for decisions about buying and selling.   _____

Q. When I gamble or play games of chance, I use a system for betting and money management.   _____

R. When I decide to put on a trade, I know I am right.   _____

S. When I decide to put on a trade, I don't believe a plan to exit is necessary.   _____

T. If I am watching CNBC and an analyst says Intel (for example) is a great buy, I will buy that stock because he or she knows more than I do.   _____

U. I plan out my activities before the start of each day.   _____

V. I am likely to go to a restaurant that serves wild   _____
    game just to try it.

W. After noticing a pattern in the market a few times,   _____
    I can trade off that pattern the next time I see it.

X. When I lose money on a trading decision, my   _____
    first thought is how to get it back.

Y. If the market is in a sideways pattern, I wait to   _____
    trade until volatility increases.

Add your score and compare with the guide in the   _____
    "Answers" section in the back of the book.

YOUR TRADING BELIEFS

The most common mistake that new traders make is to underestimate the learning curve. They find it hard to believe that—given
their experience, dedication, IQ, or whatever else they possess that
makes them special—it's unlikely they'll make any profit the first
year beyond covering their commissions and other costs. In fact, any
expectation of making money has the danger of undermining both
their discipline and their trading strategy.

Exercise 1.2

Here's a true-or-false quiz on trading beliefs. Answer these quickly,
giving your first, gut-level response. Don't contemplate what you
think the "right" answer is.

1. When I trade, my primary motivation is to make money.

    A. True

    B. False

2. The ability to take on huge amounts of risk without flinching is the top quality that all traders must possess.

   A. True

   B. False

3. One of the keys to being a good trader is to know yourself.

   A. True

   B. False

4. You need a big ego to trade—the bigger the better. Otherwise you won't have enough nerve to place a trade.

   A. True

   B. False

5. When you trade, you must make your trading decisions based on the prices you see and your technical analysis.

   A. True

   B. False

6. Focus on letting your profits run. In the end, profits will make up for any losses.

   A. True

   B. False

7. When you trade, you must be in the market as much as possible, and make as many trades as possible.

   A. True

   B. False

8. Your losing trades have more to teach you than your winning trades.

    A. True

    B. False

9. If you have a string of losing trades, step up the pace of your trade execution. Make as many trades as you can to overcome your losses quickly.

    A. True

    B. False

10. For every trader there is a holy grail, an indicator or methodology that will apply virtually every time. Finding this holy grail will measurably help to increase chances of success.

    A. True

    B. False

THE TWO BIGGEST CHALLENGES

When it comes to trading, the two biggest challenges are:

1. Losing money

2. Making money

Each of these events will cast its own web of influence over your thinking and your discipline. At all times, you must be in control of your emotions and your ego in order to make the best possible trading decisions.

LEARNING FROM LOSERS

Let's start with the losers. Here's a page out of my own recent life experience:

It was a costly error—a $110,000 error to be exact. I was trading in the S&P futures pit on a Friday morning, and I thought I had made a 50-contract trade with another trader. But it turned out that I hadn't. That trader had actually traded with someone else. By the time my clerk and I discovered the error, it was a $110,000 mistake. It's one thing to lose because of poor analysis, a mistake in timing, or some flaw in your execution. But to be right and have a six-figure loser is an indescribable frustration. I tried to battle back and did manage to cut my loss to $25,000. But even after all these years of trading, all I could think about was the fact that it would have been an $85,000 profit had it not been for that error.

It is hard to be unemotional about money. As you'll read throughout this workbook and the book it accompanies, *The Day Trader's Course*, a trader must focus on making well-executed trades and not on the money. And even after 20 years in this business, I have to tell you that this error really got to me psychologically and emotionally. For the next several trading sessions, I felt out of sync with the market. My timing was off. I was in a funk. But I traded anyway the next session, and then the session after that, and the session after that.

The market was thin. It was right before a Federal Open Market Committee (FOMC) meeting, and it was broadly anticipated that the Fed would cut rates another 50 basis points. But on the days before that meeting—as is typical when a potentially market-moving event is scheduled—the market was thin and quiet. I would have been better off on the golf course, or at least on the sidelines studying my charts.

Needless to say, that wasn't exactly a profitable time for me.

Why am I sharing this story? Because as you learn more about trading or you prepare to actually begin trading, you must understand that you will face occasional losing days, or even a string of them. You must know how to handle that risk and to avoid the dangers such as overtrading.

Overtrading is simply trading too frequently or with a larger position than market conditions warrant. Every trader falls into the overtrading trap at times. The most important thing is to recognize it and take steps immediately to correct it. When you can clear your mind, regain your composure, and focus on making well-executed trades, you'll improve your chances of getting back on track.

Here's a short exercise on dealing with losses.

Exercise 1.3

1. If you have three losing trades in a row you should:

    A. Take a break.

    B. Reexamine your technical analysis.

    C. Cut down your trading size.

    D. All of the above.

2. The problem with trading with stops is that you get taken out of the market too soon.

    A. True

    B. False

3. Making a profit on virtually all your trades is a realistic goal.

    A. True

    B. False

4. The biggest challenge for many traders is exiting a losing trade.

    A. True

    B. False

HANDLING WINNERS

I remember reading a magazine article once about lottery million-aires and how these windfall riches had ruined many of their lives. *Oh yeah,* most of us would say to ourselves. *That's a problem I'd like to have!*

But in trading, you must keep in mind that profits can skew your psychology as much as losses. The symptoms are different, of course. But the problems can be as serious. The most common "af-flictions" are:

- Believing you have the Midas touch

- Losing respect for money

With the Midas touch, you believe that everything you touch—in this case every trade you make—will turn to gold. You tell yourself that you can't lose. So you get sloppy in your preparation. You skip the market analysis one day. You trade based on your gut instinct and what you believe with happen. That's when you discover your so-called Midas touch really produces only fool's gold.

I've seen it far too many times in trading. A week of profitable days convinces a novice that he or she can master this. When that happens, you can almost guarantee a blowup. When your technical analysis and your trade execution are "on," you'll feel in sync with the market. That's when discipline is vital, to keep your mind focused and your ego in check.

Losing respect for money is a tricky thing. First of all, the goal in trading is to forget about the money when you're trading. Your focus is on making well-executed trades. In this way, you can keep fear of losing or greed to make more out of the trading equation. At the same time, you can't lose respect for money, particularly when you've had a good day.

I remember when I had my first really big day. I was having break-fast with my boss and mentor and I left the waitress the equivalent of a 233 percent tip. My generosity notwithstanding, it showed that I was getting a little full of myself. Money didn't mean as much to me after that big day as it did before—there was more where that came from! My mentor set me straight in a hurry with these words of advice: "Just because you had a big day doesn't mean you can lose respect for money. Because when you're trading, you can lose money just as fast as you got it."

Exercise 1.4

1. When you've had a big day, withdraw some of your profits from your account to reward yourself.

   A. Always

   B. Sometimes

   C. Never

2. If you've had a string of profitable trades, look to increase your trade size.

   A. True

   B. False

   C. Maybe

CRISIS OF CONFIDENCE

If you trade, eventually you will face a crisis of confidence. And if you trade long enough, you'll face many of them. If you're day trading, or you're seriously considering this endeavor, chances are you've come to this from another profession. In my 20 years of trading, I've seen people from just about every conceivable background come into the pit—doctors, psychiatrists, educators, firefighters, police officers, truck drivers, lawyers, professional athletes. I know the same can be said for screen-based traders, some of whom have left the nine-to-five world to trade on their own and others who are doing it as a second occupation.

But no matter where you come from—and regardless of whether you're a professional or a newbie, a stock or a futures trader—you will at some point face a crisis of confidence.

Here's how it usually happens: Your technical research tells you that the market is likely to move from level A up to B. But how and when that will happen is up to the market to show you. On a chart, the move from A to B may look like a straight line of possibility to you. But the market could develop a multiple-personality disorder between those two areas. It could go from A almost up to B, then reverse, retest A, break just below (or above it), then reverse again, go up to B, and then fail. Or it could go from A up to B and keep going, hitting C and then breaking sharply back down through B to A again.

As we'll discuss later, there are some hints to help you determine what the likely scenario is, but at all times you must remember:

There is more art than science when it comes to technical analysis and trading. There is no assurance that the market will go from one point to another. Nor can you rely on just one indicator, which we'll address later on in this book.

But to illustrate yet another facet of the "mental game" of trading, let's say that you've identified A as your entry point on a trade and B as your exit. You make the trade and it goes off textbook perfect. The next day, you identify a similar pattern. You pick your entry at C and your exit at D, and you put your stop in. But the market doesn't move the way it did the day before. You get stopped out, and then the market turns around and moves exactly the way you thought it would—except you're not in the market because you've been stopped out. You don't wait for the setup. You jump in, but not at an advantageous price.

Slippage is a fact of life in trading. Slippage is basically the differential between the price you see on the screen and the price at which your order is filled. In a rising market, you are likely to have a buy order filled higher than you anticipated, and in a falling one, you are likely to sell lower than you expected.

So now you're chasing the move with a less than optimal fill, and the move is stalling. If you're lucky you get out with a scratch (meaning no profit and no loss). And if you're not lucky, you've got a loser.

What happened? It could be that your own timing was off. Or perhaps the personality of the market changed—for example, from a rangebound "buy the dip" market to a more volatile one that's prone to breakouts.

You'll have this happen to you countless times if you trade. You must be prepared to handle the emotional gyrations that go along with the capriciousness of the market. More often than not, when you've been "chopped up" by the market's unexpected moves, you'll begin to lose confidence in your trading system (or at least question it) or in yourself. This is where you wonder, "Have I lost it?" or "Did I ever have it?"

Whether you're a novice or a professional, the same self-help remedies apply. (Yes, you'll reexamine your trading strategies, your trade setups, and your technical analysis techniques. But first you must take a look inside—because that's where trading begins.)

1. Reflect upon the successful trades you've made, the good decisions you've made, and how your process works. Overall, reflect on the good that you've gained from trading.

2. Take a look at yourself, at your personal life. Is there something going on in your life—positive or negative—that interferes with your trading decisions? Maybe you're buying a new house or there's a new baby in your family. Maybe you're going through a difficult personal time, from a death or serious illness in the family to the breakup of a significant relationship. When you have emotional upheaval in your life, know that it will potentially affect your trading. Thus you might want to reduce your trading size, or even sit out some days, until you have a better mental equilibrium.

3. Have you lost respect for money? While you shouldn't make money your primary motivation, you mustn't lose respect for it.

Contemplate all the things that money buys in your life, or go out and spend some on yourself or your family. That should bring home the value of a dollar.

4. At this point, you can look at the losing trades you've made. (Don't rush this step and dive into this analysis without the perspective gained in steps 1 through 3.) Did you buy at the top because you were chasing the market? Did you hang on to losers too long? What would you do differently now with the benefit of hindsight?

5. Go back to the favorite type of trade that you make, the one that has a high probability of being a winner. Now, execute that trade for a profit. Don't swing for the fences. Try to hit a single—just a small profit. Take baby steps as you trade, slowly, deliberately, and with discipline, to regain your composure and your confidence.

Next chapter . . . Getting Started

2

Getting Started

You're ready to trade . . . but how do you start? At the risk of sounding overly simplistic, it's vital to start at the beginning—with how your trade is executed. When you are trading for the first time—be it stocks or futures—there are more important considerations than just the commission price that you're going to pay. Far more important are:

- *Reliability.* Whether you trade electronically or through a broker, you must be assured of reliability on entering orders, trade execution, and confirmation.

- *Full-service versus discount broker.* Know what you're paying for—or not. A full-service broker provides a certain amount of hand-holding, from market insights to advice on execution, in return for a full-service commission. A discount broker offers no advice per se, but there should be a backup—particularly for an electronic order entry—should you encounter a problem with an order.

- *What the price includes.* Does the commission rate you're quoted cover all costs? For futures, is it based on a roundturn, meaning in the trade and out? Are there extra fees for clearing?

17

In stocks, does the low commission rate apply only to trades or accounts of a certain size?

For both stocks and futures, there are three basic types of brokerage services:

1. *Full-service broker.* Typically offers some advice and trade-execution assistance in return for a higher commission.

2. *Discount brokerage.* Offers fewer services, but a lower commission rate, than the full-service broker.

3. *Direct access.* Enables you to enter your orders directly into the marketplace. In stocks, direct access is typically utilized by self-directed (meaning no broker support) traders/investors who actively trade stocks. With direct access, stock traders can route their orders to any of a number of electronic communications networks (ECNs), to a Small Order Execution System (SOES) for Nasdaq stocks, or a brokerage's automated routing system. In futures, orders are transmitted via the Internet directly to the floor of the futures exchange. Depending on the contract, orders may be routed to an electronic trading platform (such as the Chicago Mercantile Exchange's Globex for S&P and Nasdaq e-minis) or to a trading desk on the floor. In some cases, orders that must be executed in the pit (such as S&P and Nasdaq majors) are transmitted to brokers in the pit who carry handheld computers.

Exercise 2.1

1. When you trade stocks online, you have essentially a direct connection to the securities market.

   A. True

   B. False

2. The price you see on the screen when you execute a trade is the price you'll get.

    A. True

    B. False

3. With online stock trading, your broker has several choices of how to route your trade for execution.

    A. True

    B. False

4. Brokers may offer the option—but not the guarantee—of filling orders at a better price if possible.

    A. True

    B. False

5. ECNs—electronic communications networks—are electronic trading platforms offered by the major stock exchanges, such as Nasdaq and the New York Stock Exchange.

    A. True

    B. False

6. With direct access for stock trading, you may pick where your order is executed.

    A. True

    B. False

7. In futures trading, your broker can take the other side of your trade (i.e., buying the contracts you're offering for sale or selling what you want to buy).

    A. True

    B. False

BEFORE YOU BEGIN

No one starts out trading believing they will lose. However, statistically speaking, there is a greater likelihood of failure than success. For example, did you know that the average "life span" of a day trader is six months? Did you know that for every 10 people who try their hands at trading, three will survive the first year? And that of those three, maybe one will be able to make a decent living?

If you don't take these cold hard facts to heart, you could very well become one of the unfortunate statistics.

Before you open a trading account, here is a checklist to consider:

- Make sure you fully understand the language of the risk disclosure statements that you'll be asked to sign. Be honest with yourself about your financial situation, your knowledge of and experience in the markets, and your emotional and psychological makeup—particularly when it comes to handling loss.

- When you open a discount trading account, it may be assumed that you have enough trading experience to make your own trading decisions. With most discount trading and all direct-access trading, no one is going to hold your hand and walk you through a trade. You and you alone will be managing your position—the entry and exit points and stop placement—and your risk.

- Paper trading may be helpful to practice certain aspects of trade execution. However, paper trading cannot replicate the emotional and psychological aspects of trading, slippage on fills, or real-time market conditions.

- Trading commissions—even discounted commissions—can erode your trading capital. Calculate commissions into your trading strategy before adopting a day trading method and making frequent trades.

- Trading involves the risk of substantial loss of capital. Use only speculative capital to trade. This means money that you could lose without impacting your lifestyle or livelihood.

- Electronic order-entry systems fail regularly, causing delay or the inability to fill an order.

- If you trade futures, understand the impact of leverage. It's possible, for example, to trade one S&P mini contract (with an approximate current value of $62,500 with S&P futures at 1300) with as little as $5,000 in your account. But any losses that you might incur are based on the $62,500 value of the contract, and not the $5,000 in your account.

Exercise 2.2

1. Paper trading can be helpful in:

   A. Watching the market real-time.

   B. Determining entry and exit points.

   C. Determining stop levels.

   D. All of the above.

2. When you paper trade, ignore the false starts and dumb mistakes that you make, and focus only on the well-executed trades that you identify.

   A. True

   B. False

3. Paper trading is worthless.

   A. True

   B. False

4. To open a trading account, I must have a minimum of $25,000.

   A. True

   B. False

5. It's easy to get a margin account for stock trading.

   A. True

   B. False

6. If I trade stocks on 2-to-1 margin, the brokerage firm will absorb losses on its half of the trade.

   A. True

   B. False

One of the common questions that wanna-be traders ask is, "How do I know what to do?" That, as they say, is the $1 million question! Your trading strategy will depend on many factors, including:

- The prevailing price

- Market analysis and sentiment

- Trading style and parameters

- Experience in the market

To trade effectively, you must use real-time quotes. Delayed quotes that are available free of charge from many web sites are useful only to the buy-and-hold investor for whom a 20-minute delay is not material. Some professional traders use two independent sources of quotes in case of a transmission error or a glitch in the data stream.

Quotes will be displayed in any number of charting programs, which your data vendor may very likely provide. As discussed in further chapters, you may use a combination of daily and intraday charts of varying time frames. Using the charts, with technical analysis (as we'll discuss in later chapters) you can help determine the market sentiment and likely price targets of upcoming moves.

Your trading style and parameters will depend on many factors, including your own objectives and experience, and the time you have to devote daily to the market. As a rule of thumb, if you are trading on the side it is virtually impossible to day trade, meaning enter and exit positions intraday. If you have a day job you will not have the time or attention span to devote to day trading. Rather, you may want to take short-term trades in the direction of the prevailing momentum, also known as swing trading. Even as a full-time trader, you may want to do either day trading or short-term trading (or a combination of both), depending on your style.

In general, short-term trading seeks to take advantage of larger moves in the market and can tolerate (based on your risk and trading parameters) comparatively larger moves, which will also impact your stop placement. Day trading is typically aimed at smaller moves or a series of smaller moves made intraday.

Your experience in the market speaks for itself. Many traders have evolved from active investors who managed portfolios and made longer-term stock trades, moved to shorter-term stock trades, and then graduated to day trading in stocks and stock index futures. Do not rush your learning curve. Only you can judge when you feel sufficiently comfortable in the dynamics of whatever market you're trading to increase your frequency of trading or to become more aggressive in the market.

ORDER TYPES

When you're trading, there are many types of orders that you can use to enter and exit your trade. Here is a brief explanation of various order types:

Market order: An order to be executed immediately at the prevailing market price.

Limit order: An order that can be executed only at a specified price or better.

Day order: An order that automatically expires if it is not executed on that day.

Open order: An order that remains in force until canceled or until the contract expires. This may also be known as a good-til-canceled (GTC) order.

Spread order: An order to buy one contract and sell a different contract simultaneously, at a quoted differential.

Stop order: An order that becomes a market order only when the market trades at a specified price. This may also be called a stop loss order, enabling a trader to exit a losing position at a specified price for a predetermined loss. A stop order may be a good-til-canceled order or any other form of time-limit order.

- A stop order to buy must always be executed when the buy price is at or above the stop price.

- A stop order to sell must always be executed when the sell price is at or below the stop price.

Stop limit order: An order that becomes a limit order (to be filled at a specified price or better) when the market trades at a specified price.

Market-on-close order: A market order that is executed at the closing price. If it's not executed, the order is canceled.

Market-if-touched order: A price order that becomes a market order when the market trades at a specific price at least once.

Order-cancels-other order: Includes two orders, one of which cancels the other when filled. This may also be called a one-cancels-other order.

(Traders sometimes joke about another type of "order" used by nervous novice traders. They call it "CIC" or "cancel if close"—as in, "I think the market is going there and I'll put an order in, but I'd better cancel it if the market gets close to that.")

Exercise 2.3

1. The market just broke above key resistance, and the next target is several ticks away. You want to enter the market immediately. You would most likely use a:

    A. Price order

    B. Market order

    C. Limit order

2. S&P futures have traded off the intraday high of 1308 and are moving below 1300, where you believe there is solid support. You'd like to be a buyer at 1300 or better. You would most likely use a:

    A. Market order

    B. Price order

    C. Limit order

3. You establish a short position at 1309.50, and the market is moving down. You technical analysis shows support at 1301.50. To exit the short position profitably, you'd most likely enter a:

    A. Market order

    B. Stop loss order

    C. Price order

4. You see key support at 1298 and expect the market to trade steadily higher from that level. After the market hits 1298 and

trades slightly higher, you enter with a market order at 1298.40. The market meets unexpected resistance at 1299—far short of your profit target at 1301.50—and begins to sell off. What kind of orders would protect you and your position the best?

INFORMATION

When you're trading, watching the prices as they're displayed real-time on your screen, it's important that you know what's happening in the world around you. Watching prices tick up and down all day can give you a feeling of isolation or a kind of myopia in which you feel that times and prices are all that exists. The market, however, does not move in a vacuum. A variety of external events impacts the market. There may be a regularly scheduled economic report. Or perhaps there is an unexpected announcement, such as an earnings warning by a major company or a surprise rate cut (or hike) by the Federal Reserve. If you're trading, you need to know what's going on.

Many traders tune into a financial television network to learn the news of the day and also be informed of sudden news as it breaks. Further, these networks frequently interview company chief executives, economists, and analysts who may provide some insight into market dynamics. In addition, your quote provider may also offer a news package that allows you to display scrolling headlines on your screen. Many data packages can be manipulated to show any news headlines or announcements on a particular company, group of companies, or sector.

Having real-time information and the ability to interpret and use it is vital to a trader's success.

A recent study from the University of California at Davis examined the trading behaviors and performance of 1,607 investors who switched from trading with a broker over the phone to online trading from 1991 to 1996.

The study, "Online Investors: Do the Slow Die First?" yielded some very interesting conclusions:

- Those who switched to online trading did so after an "unusually strong performance prior to going online," beating the market by more than 2 percent per year.

- After going online, they tended to trade "more actively, more speculatively, and less profitably than before." The result was they lagged the market by more than 3 percent per year.

What's going on here? As the study notes, you'd think that lower trading costs, improved execution speed, and greater ease of access would have helped these online traders. Rather, the study found, the increase in trading activity and the decrease in performance by online investors were due to several important factors: overconfidence, the illusion of knowledge, and the illusion of control.

The study is enlightening for several reasons. As we all know, the evolution in trading (both stocks and futures) has been from placing trades through a broker on the phone to online trading. In stocks, at first this was essentially a faster way to e-mail your broker, since the order received via online transmission still had to be executed by a person. Now, direct access—whereby a trader can choose how his or her trade is routed—is the preferred venue.

But you can't jump into direct-access trading any more than you can jump into trading in general. Whether you're trading futures or stocks, the importance of maintaining discipline and self-control can't be overemphasized.

There is a risk here for any of us traders if we shrug off the findings of this study and say, "Well, investors (a disparaging term) would think that." After all, traders are just as apt to fall prey to overtrading and the illusion of control and knowledge as investors. In fact, we traders may be even more prone to it. Why? Because we live and breathe this market, so we feel somehow we're intuitively in touch with it. This gives a feeling of knowing what's going to happen next that may not be grounded in reality (as in constantly monitoring the market action and studying the charts). Or you may feel so in control that you are taken by surprise by a sudden move in the market (Fed cut, news headline, whatever).

Exercise 2.4

1. If you have real-time market data and information, you have an advantage in the marketplace.

    A. True

    B. False

2. If you are going to trade, you must know what is going on in every market, in every industrial sector, at any given time.

    A. True

    B. False

Coming up . . . Technical Analysis 101

3

Technical Analysis 101

Technical analysis is the study of the market based on price movements, volume, trends, and patterns. The basic premise of technical analysis is that the market's past can help in determining the likely path it will take in the future. But how do you do that?

In this overview of the basics of technical analysis, it's important to start at the proverbial beginning, and not rush through any steps. The exercises are designed to help you to recognize and interpret chart patterns and indicators.

CHART PATTERNS

Looking at a chart is a little like finding constellations in the night sky. At first, in Figure 3.1, you just see separate points. But with concentration, a pattern will emerge.

When you look at the chart, what features stand out? It may be helpful at first to forget that this is a chart of prices, and only look for the picture that emerges. If you could compare the line on this chart (or on any chart, for that matter) to a landscape, where would you find peaks resembling those of a mountain range? Where are the valleys?

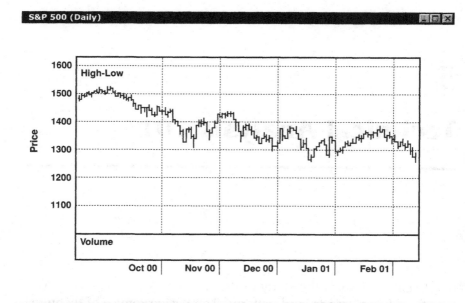

Figure 3.1   S&P 500 I (Daily) (*Source:* www.dtnfs.com, DTN Financial Services)

As simplistic as this sounds, it is important to focus only on the chart pattern—and not on the interpretation—at this point. If you try to rush through these initial steps, you risk losing a key acclimation to the chart. If you're already familiar with some of the basics of technical analysis, you could feel like you're reinventing the wheel at this point. Just bear with it (and keep in mind that if Henry Ford had felt as if he were reinventing the wheel because both Daimler and Benz had beaten him to production, then he might never have made his innovations or perfected the assembly line!).

At this point, relate the peaks and valleys of the chart patterns to the market. (While we use a chart of S&P futures in this example, *any* chart of *any* stock, commodity, or futures contract can be used—as long as it is based on price and time data.)

Exercise 3.1

1. In Figure 3.1, how does the first peak correlate with the market?

2. Look at the entire chart. What are some of the noticeable features?

These chart patterns are more than just pictures. They can be used to help interpret or project where the market is likely to be headed. This is because moves in the market tend to be symmetrical. That symmetry, however, may not be a perfect up and down move. Rather, the symmetry may be in *time* or *price*.

- Time symmetry refers to an up move and a down move that take place over equivalent periods of time—although the starting and ending prices may be different.

- Price symmetry refers to an up move and a down move that begin and end at equivalent prices, although the time involved in each move may be shorter or longer.

Looking at a chart of previous market activity, it is easier to see the symmetry. However, this becomes more difficult when you're studying the market live. To replicate this, start with a fresh chart (any chart of your own choosing, of any stock, stock index, or commodity).

1. Cover the chart completely with a blank piece of paper.

2. Move the blank piece of paper (the covering sheet) an inch to the right. What do you see thus far? Is the market moving higher or lower?

3. Move the covering sheet another inch to the right. Now what do you see? What is the market direction? Do you see a possible top or bottom (peak or valley) forming?

4. Move the sheet by inches across the sheet. If you see what appears to be a significant price point, mark it on the chart. Then

uncover more of the chart. Mark other significant points as they are revealed.

5. When the entire chart is uncovered, look at how well (or how poorly) you did at marking or identifying the significant points along the way.

6. Repeat the process with other charts.

Charts can cover a few minutes or many years. Each bar may represent a minute or a month. Each chart and each scale has something significant to tell. How applicable that information is to your trading style depends, of course, on your trading style.

Exercise 3.2

1. A short-term trader would use daily charts but not intraday charts.

    A. True

    B. False

2. A day trader—who enters and exits a trade intraday and often within hours or even minutes—would use only intraday charts.

    A. True

    B. False

USING CHARTS

Looking at your chart in the previous exercise—and with the benefit of hindsight—determine where you would buy and where you would sell, as well as where you would put your stop. Obviously, the goal of all trading is to "buy low, sell high." But remember there is an underlying rule that must not be violated: "Protect your capital to come back and trade another day." That is the purpose of using a stop. A stop is the exit point for a losing trade. This stop is placed at a predetermined level at the same time you execute your trade. For example, if you go long a stock at $20 for what you see as a quick run to $20.75, you might put your sell stop (to exit the trade should the market move against you) at $19.75 or $19.60.

Remember, when trading there are *two possible points* at which to exit your trade.

1. Your profit target—whether you're trading from the long side or the short side.

2. Your stop placement at a predetermined loss level should the market turn against you.

Granted, as we'll discuss in depth later, you may decide to scale out of a position profitably at your initial target and then subsequent targets. But when you place your trade, you know where you will exit profitably and where you will exit in case of a loss. Your technical analysis will help you to determine all of those points.

Now, get a fresh chart of any stock, stock index, or commodity.

1. Cover the chart completely.

2. Move the covering sheet to the right, exposing a small amount of price data.

3. As you move the covering sheet, mark where you'd buy and where you'd sell, as well as where you would place your stop.

4. When the chart is completely uncovered, see how well (or poorly) you did in determining buy and sell points, based only on the pattern of the chart.

USING STOPS

Stops act like a safety net, preventing a fall beyond a danger point. Where you place your stop will depend on many factors, including:

- The duration of your trade

- Your risk tolerance

For day trading, specifically, the objective is to exit a losing trade quickly, before losses mount. After exiting the trade, you can then reassess your trading strategy and reenter the market when opportunities are presented.

Exercise 3.3

1. While it's important to trade with stops, they can be "mental stops" and do not have to be entered as stop orders.

   A. True

   B. False

2. The problem with stops is that you get stopped out of the market too soon—just as the market is about to turn around and go your way.

   A. True

   B. False

3. Stops can also be used to enter the market, not just to exit positions.

   A. True

   B. False

THE IMPORTANCE OF STOPS

Stops are vital to any trading plan to limit losses, but they also perform another function: They confirm a trader's discipline. Without discipline, as I've said countless times and will say countless more, you have little (if any) chance of being consistent in your trading. Stops also are an antidote to a fairly common syndrome among new traders: the "wishing, hoping, and praying" syndrome.

Despite what you'd believe—particularly when the market is moving against you and you've been foolish enough to trade without a stop—there is no use wishing, hoping, or praying for the market to turn around. Now, everybody knows this. But when you're in the thick of the market battle, it's easy to lose your focus, your discipline, and ultimately your capital.

Take a friend of mine, whom we'll call "Trader Joe." He was a successful businessman who in the midst of a career change decided to try trading. I had warned him that trading would take time to master, just as he had built his business over time. But he didn't want to go through the inevitable one-year learning curve, during which he should expect just to cover expenses. His impatient attitude encouraged him to trade with too much risk and too little discipline.

Without any rhyme or reason (or technical analysis to back it up), Trader Joe bought two S&P major contracts, we'll say at 1373. The market immediately broke 1,000 points. (That's 1,000 pit points, or 10.00 on the screen.) At 1363, Joe was out about $5,000. Hoping to make up for that loss, Joe bought two more contracts and prayed that the market would go up. Instead, it fell another 1,000 points to 1353, which was limit down. At that point, he was out $10,000 on the two-lot from 1373 and out $5,000 on the two-lot from 1363. With the market locked limit—meaning it had reached the initial down limit and trading was halted temporarily—he couldn't sell those contracts even if he did want to take the $15,000 loss. When the market reopened after the limit expired, he figured this *had* to be the bottom. So he bought another contract. The market traded higher momentarily, and then broke another 1,000 points to 1343.

With a total loss at this point of $27,500, he was too stunned to move. Then slowly the market began to turn around and ended up rallying, all the way to 1363, at which he sold all five contracts. He made $2,500 on the one-lot from 1353, scratched the two-lot from 1363, and lost $5,000 on the two-lot from 1373, for a net loss over-all of $2,500. Disaster averted.

"What were you thinking?" I scolded Trader Joe as if he were a five-year-old.

"All I wanted to do," Trader Joe said sheepishly, "was find the computer room at the exchange and pull the plug on the market quotes to keep it from going down any further!"

You might chuckle at the Trader Joe story, but be warned. If you trade without stops or if you cancel stops because you don't want to be stopped out of a trade yet again, you may face mounting losses. And in the end, you may not be as lucky as Trader Joe was. For him, the market ended up rallying and bailed him out of a hole. But it could have just as easily gone the other way, and the loss could have gotten even bigger.

MOVING AVERAGES

Thus far, we've looked only at the chart to determine buy, sell, and stop points. These are the very basics of technical analysis to disci-pline yourself to use the chart as the map by which you will navigate the market. Once you've become comfortable with looking at the chart, it's time to add the first indicator. One of the most widely used indicators is the moving average.

A moving average is based on the average of prices for a specific period of time. For example, a 200-day moving average is the aver-age of settlement prices for the previous 200 days; the 50-day mov-ing average covers the previous 50 days, and so on. Moving averages—like charts themselves—can be applied to virtually any time frame. You can have a 10-day moving average on a daily chart, or a 10-minute moving average on an intraday chart. Keep in mind that the shorter the time frame, the more responsive a moving average is likely to be. In other words, a 10-day moving average is more likely to track the movement of the current market than the 200-day moving average.

However, every moving average has the potential to tell you something about the market.

Exercise 3.4

In Figure 3.2, notice the correlation between the market (or the price line as we'll call it) and the 200-day moving average.

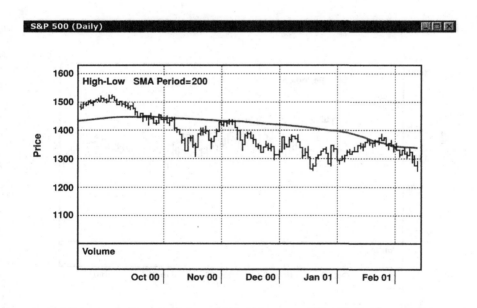

Figure 3.2 S&P 500 I (Daily) (*Source:* www.dtnfs.com, DTN Financial Services)

1. What stands out the most as you look at the chart and the 200-day moving average?

2. Examine the relationship between the 200-day moving average and the market. What happens when the market touches or crosses the moving average? Observing what the market *has done* in these circumstances will help you recognize probable patterns and market behavior in the future.

   Now look at Figure 3.3 of the S&P 500 cash market with a 20-day moving average.

3. What stands out the most as you look at this chart and the 20-day moving average?

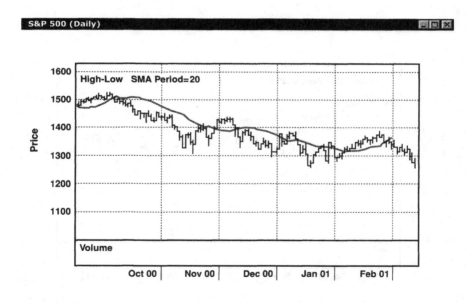

Figure 3.3 S&P 500 I (Daily) (*Source:* www.dtnfs.com, DTN Financial Services)

As a trader, your goal will be to find the moving average that most closely matches your trading style. One rule of thumb is that the longer your time frame, the longer the time frame for the moving average that you'll use; the shorter your time frame, the shorter the moving average you'll use. But all moving averages potentially have something to tell you about the market's dynamics.

4. If you're day trading, the 200-day moving average lags the market too much to be meaningful for your strategy.

   A. True

   B. False

5. You should not use any more than three moving averages as part of your strategy.

   A. True

   B. False

6. Finding the right moving averages to use is a process of trial and error.

   A. True

   B. False

When you look at a chart with moving averages, it's fairly easy to see which ones track the market closely. But this is not the end result of your search. Rather, you are looking for the moving average that will cross the price line of your chart at key points, indicating buys and sells. To illustrate, follow these steps.

1. Choose a chart of any stock or index.

2. Apply the first moving average to the line, say the 200-day moving average. Does the price line touch or cross the moving average at any point? If so, what does the market do when the moving average is touched or crossed?

3. Repeat this pattern with increasingly short-term moving averages. Does the 50-day moving average touch or cross the moving average at any point? If so, what does the market do then?

4. Apply the 20-day moving average, and repeat the observation process.

Your goal is to find a moving average that helps you to predict when the market will make a significant move. In other words, you are looking for a moving average that presents key resistance to the market (if the price line is below) or key support (if the price line is above). What happens when the market crosses the line? Does the upside or downside accelerate?

TREND LINES

When you look at a chart, it's fairly easy to see when the market was moving (trending) higher, when it was going sideways (range-bound), and when it was going (trending) lower. As a trader, real-time, the challenge will be to gauge the trend and anticipate when it might reverse.

One way is to look at the trend lines. The easiest comparison might be to think of these as the path that the market should follow if there were no fundamental or technical changes. For example:

1. Start with a chart of any stock or index.

2. Identify two key points: either two consecutive highs or two consecutive lows.

3. Draw a line between those two points (two highs or two lows) and extend the line out into the future.

The line drawn between the two highs shows a resistance level at that time (which the market may later trade above). The line drawn between the two lows shows a support level (which the market may later trade below).

As with moving averages, there are many possible trend lines that can be drawn. Similarly, you may apply trend lines to intraday, daily, weekly, monthly, or yearly charts.

The objective is to find a trend line that is relevant to the market right now, real-time, and within your trading parameters. If you're taking a short-term position over a few days, you will want to identify trends that would help you locate key support or resistance that would be applicable for several days. If you're day trading, you will want to identify trends for an ultra-short-term position that might last a few hours or even minutes.

Another type of trend line can be drawn between a significant high and a significant low. To be meaningful, however, the lines must connect a high and a low that occur in *different but consecutive price patterns.*

1. Start with a chart of any stock or index in which there are at least two price patterns, such as an uptrend and a downtrend, or an uptrend or downtrend with a rangebound (sideways) pattern.

2. Pick a significant high from one price pattern and a significant low from another price pattern. Draw a line between the two points and extend them into the future.

3. Choose a significant low from one price pattern and a significant high from the other and draw a line, extending into the future.

What do those lines show? Does the price line subsequently touch, cross, approach, or veer away from these lines?

Exercise 3.5

1. What is the purpose of a trend line?

2. Trend lines that connect three or more significant high or low points are more important than those that connect only two.

    A. True

    B. False

3. Define a rangebound market.

   A. A quiet, slow market with little activity.

   B. A market in which there are no significant new highs and no significant new lows.

   C. A market that stays between the 10-day and 50-day moving averages.

4. What happens when the market is making lower highs and higher lows?

   A. Trending

   B. Contraction

   C. Reversal

5. What typically happens after a formation described in the preceding question?

   A. Breakout

   B. Reversal

   C. Follow-through

   The market never stays in one trend forever. And the shorter time frames may display their own trends. A market could trend higher one day and lower then next, but still have an upward (or downward) bias for the longer term.

   A period of contraction—lower highs and higher lows, as just described—is the transition time before a breakout into a new trend. Here's one way to analyze a contracting market.

1. Draw a line connecting the lower highs, touching two or more of the high points.

2. Draw a line connecting the higher lows, touching two or more of the high points.

3. The line formed by the highs will slope downward. The line formed by the lows will slope upward.

4. Extend these lines out into the future until they cross. This will form a triangle pattern.

   Roughly three-quarters of the way along that triangle is the typical breakout point from the contraction. Often the direction that the market takes after the breakout is the same as the one it had before the contraction began.

Remember, technical analysis, like trading, is not an exact science. There is no formula that can be applied every time, and there are many variables—conflicting and confirming—that go into market dynamics. The most important thing is to look at what each feature and indicator is telling you, and apply that to the broader picture.

Coming up . . . Technical Analysis 102

4

Technical Analysis 102

The premise of technical analysis is that indications of future prices are contained in past price patterns. One example of this premise is a trend line, which was discussed in the previous workbook chapter. To recap, a trend line is drawn between significant highs or significant lows. The resulting trend lines, when extended, delineate support and resistance based on that price pattern. To build upon this concept, a trader can use support and resistance lines to form a trend channel.

TREND CHANNELS

Within a single price formation (an uptrend, a downtrend, or a rangebound pattern), trend channels can be drawn by connecting two or more highs (the top of the channel) and two or more lows (the bottom of the channel). These channel lines then define the outer boundaries of the price pattern. If the trend continues, the prices should stay within these boundaries. If the trend breaks in one direction or another, the prices will cross the channel lines.

1. Start with a chart of any stock or index.

2. Mark trend channels by connecting significant highs and then significant lows.

If the prices are trending upward, the channel lines also will trend upward. If prices are trending downward, the channel lines also will trend downward. In a sideways pattern, the channel lines will be roughly horizontal.

Looking at subsequent real-time prices, what happens when the market approaches the trend lines? Does the market attempt to break through one line or the other? What happens when the market touches these lines?

Remember that the market will eventually reach a resistance level at which buyers will become more aggressive enabling the market to move higher or a support level at which sellers will dominate, and the the market will move lower. Traders must be alert for these trend changes.

MOVING AVERAGE ENVELOPE

Another way to plot the "outer limits" of the market is to use moving average envelopes. A moving average, as discussed in the previous *Workbook* chapter, depicts the average of prices for a specific period of time. With a moving average envelope, lines are plotted above and below, based on a specific percentage extension from the moving average.

As with every facet of technical analysis, a lot depends on trial and error to find (in this case) the moving average percentage envelope that best fits the current trading conditions.

1. Start with a chart of any stock or index. Add a moving average of any length of time.

2. Apply a percentage envelope. (Most trading software programs will allow you to do this.) Start with a small percentage such as 0.5 percent or 1 percent. See where the envelope lines are drawn. How do they relate to the highs and lows that you observe?

3. If the highs and lows surpass these envelope lines, then increase the percentage. Now how does this new envelope relate to the highs and lows?

The objective is to find the percentage envelope that best defines the limits of the highs and lows.

Once you have defined the limits of the current highs and lows, you can observe what happens when the market approaches these limits in real time. Will these lines pose support and/or resistance? Or have the market dynamics changed, so that these limits might be exceeded in one direction or the other?

CHART PATTERNS

Technical analysis is far more than looking for the X that marks the spot. But occasionally there are signs that you can look for—although they are far more likely to be W's, M's, U's and V's!

At the risk of stating the obvious, it's important to remember that the chart itself and the patterns that are formed are visual representations of market activity. Here's a brief overview:

Exercise 4.1

1. What is an uptrend defined by?

2. What is a downtrend defined by?

3. What is the change in a trend called?

Just as these trends can be defined in words, they are also recognizable on a chart, especially in hindsight after a trend has been established. As your study of technical analysis continues, you'll be looking for other formations to help you determine what the market is likely to do next.

One of the common patterns that traders look for is a U or V that signals a reversal. Essentially, the U and the V are the same formation, only the first forms a more gradual bottom and the second makes a bottom and reverses more dramatically (sharply).

Keep in mind that, as discussed earlier, the market tends to make symmetrical moves. If a market is going downward, you'd expect that at some point it will turn and make an upward move. This symmetry can be found on a short-term scale and a longer-term scale. (To view this, look at a 10-day chart of a stock or index and then a 6-month or 12-month chart of the same stock or index. Examples of symmetry most likely will be found in both charts, and there will be "symmetry within the symmetry." You may find that the market is making a broad, cup-shaped formation over the long term, and within that are many smaller U's that are visible on a short-term chart.)

Exercise 4.2

1. Looking at Figure 4.1, what feature stands out to you? What would that indicate to you?

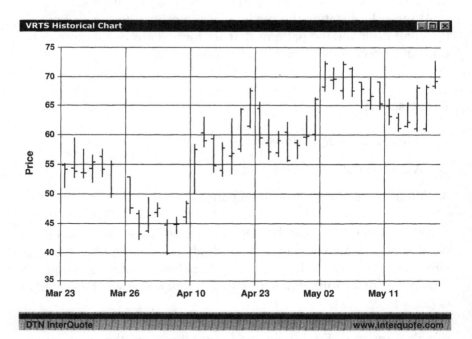

Figure 4.1 VRTS Historical Chart (Veritas) (*Source:* www.interquote.com, DTN Financial Services)

2. Looking at this same chart, are there other, smaller features that also stand out?

When it comes to chart formations, it is far easier to see them in hindsight than when the market is live. On a real-time basis, what you will be looking for is an indication that a downtrend will reach a critical support level at which the market will make a bottom and then move to the upside.

- Moves in the market tend to be symmetrical. Thus, if the market had a slow but steady decline you'd expect the same kind of incline on the other side.

- The market does not move in one direction forever. Eventually, it will turn and go the other way.

- Within larger patterns, there will be smaller patterns.

- Trend lines, support and resistance levels, and the market's behavior at key price levels will help to determine the kind of pattern that is being formed.

M's AND W's

Other chart formations that are recognized fairly easily are M's and W's. These are also known, respectively, as "double tops" and "double bottoms."

An M is formed when the market makes a high, sells off, then makes a second high at or near the first level, and then fails again. This is known as a "failed retest of the highs."

A W is formed when the market makes a low, rebounds, then makes a second low at or near the first level, and then rallies. This is known as a "failed retest of the lows."

Exercise 4.3

Figure 4.2 shows an M formation in BEA Software (BEAS), from mid-April through early May. You may find it difficult at first to see this formation right away. Don't be discouraged. It takes time and practice to recognize these patterns. In this chart, your eyes may have focused first on the V that was formed on April 6. If so, that's a good thing! *All* observation is relevant when it comes to chart patterns. A good deal of technical analysis has to do with observation—literally, just looking at what stands out at first, and then what you discover as you continue to look at a chart.

1. As you look at the M formation (from mid-April to the first peak over $45 a share, down to near $35 a share thereafter, and a sec-

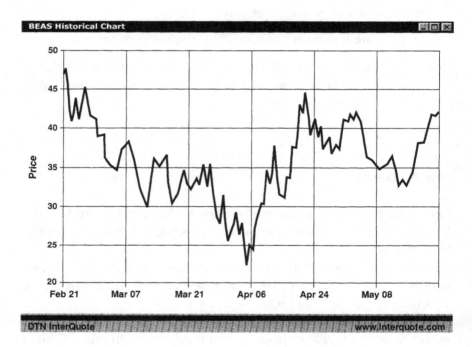

Figure 4.2   BEAS Historical Chart (BEA Systems Inc.) (*Source:* www.interquote.com, DTN Financial Services)

ond peak around $43 a share in late April, followed by the low in early May), what features stand out?

2. How did the market react after the second peak of the M was made?

3. What relevance will the price levels of the M pattern have going forward?

Similarly, a W—as a failed retest of the lows—is significant because it confirms support at or near the lows. In other words, despite a second attempt to reach or exceed the lows, the market could not break that level.

- Search through charts of your own choosing. Look for M and W patterns.

- As you would expect, does the market sell off sharply after the second peak of an M, or does it rally noticeably after the second valley of the W?

- If the market retests the peaks of the M or the valleys of the W you would expect significant resistance or support, respectively.

THE KISS PRINCIPLE FOR TECHNICAL ANALYSIS

Undoubtedly you've heard of the KISS principle—"Keep it simple, stupid." For a student of technical analysis, there is wisdom in KISS. Too many times, traders rush into more complicated factors of technical analysis—using all the bells and whistles on their software programs—without understanding the basics. Even if you subscribe to a service that provides you with technical analysis (one that tells you there is a "double top" at a price level, or "solid support" somewhere else, etc.) you should still be able to recognize basic patterns on a chart.

Trading can be very subjective. There is no denying certain things like the price level of a contract high or the 52-week price range of a stock. These are immutable facts. But in between these price facts there are a lot of interpretations. Even in the rally we saw early in the second quarter of 2001 there have been two strong opinions about what had really taken place. There were those who believed this was it: The market turned around, the bottom was in place, and we were off to the races. Others believed that this was a pause in a market that is still dominated by the bears. And, there were the middle-of-the-roaders who believe this market will have a lot of false starts before it decides which direction it will take (which as of July 2001 appears to be the case).

This confluence of opinion—bullish, bearish, and in-between—is what makes up a marketplace. Two traders can look at the same scenario and derive two entirely different opinions. And, they can both be correct! One trader with a short-term view may see Stock X as a buy today at a certain price level, with a profit objective a few ticks higher that is expected to be reached the same day. Another trader may wait for that higher price point to be reached to short the stock for a position trade to anticipated lower levels. Two opinions. Two strategies. Two time frames.

In this discussion of technical analysis, I've purposely focused on the basics. Too many times traders gloss over the beginning because they want to get to the "good stuff" later on. The problem is, without a firm foundation in the basics of technical analysis, the more complex indicators and methodologies will not be as useful. In fact, you could end up confusing yourself because indicators *can* be conflicting. You must take into account the fuller picture of the market. In other words, when you're trading you have to consider both the proverbial forest and the individual trees.

There are many other indicators—in addition to the ones discussed thus far—that you may eventually incorporate into your analysis. Many software programs include these and other indicators. Each time you add an indicator to your trading methodology, the same practice applies:

1. Start with a just a chart—no trend lines, moving averages, or other indicators. And just observe. What do you see? Train your

eye and your mind to pick out the basic patterns discussed thus far—the V's, U's, M's, W's, contracting triangles, and so forth.

2. Now apply the indicator to your chart. See how it applies to the previous price activity. For example, does the indicator match up with the high of the M pattern or the low of the V or U? Adjust the parameters of the indicator, taking in more or less time. Now how does it match up with the real-time price line?

3. One by one, add the indicators that you've been using—the trend lines, trend channels, moving averages, and so forth. Is there a consensus of opinion among the indicators?

Additional indicators include:

*   ***Stochastics:*** The stochastic oscillator compares the closing price with the price range for a given time period. The premise is that in an uptrend the closes tend to be near the high and in a downtrend the closes tend to be near the low. The stochastic oscillator is plotted on a chart with values from 0 to 100 for a specific time frame. The oscillator is displayed as two lines: The "%K" line is based on the high, the low, and the close. The "%D" is a moving average of the "%K" line. In general, stochastic readings at 80 or above are considered strong and indicate that the price is closing near its high. Readings below 20 are also considered strong but they indicate that the price is closing near its low.

*   ***Relative Strength Index (RSI):*** This technical indicator helps to gauge the strength of the price of a stock or index vis-à-vis its past performance. It is based largely on the premise that the RSI will top out or bottom out before the market makes its actual top or bottom. Thus, the RSI is watched by many traders for a signal that a reversal could be developing. RSI readings above 70 are usually interpreted as overbought and readings below 30 indicate oversold. RSI, like moving averages, can be applied to various time frames. In general, the shorter the time frame the more volatile the RSI.

- **Bollinger Bands:** These trading bands are plotted at standard deviation levels above and below a moving average. The bands typically widen during volatile markets and contract during calmer periods. With Bollinger Bands, the assumption is that prices tend to stay within the upper and lower bands. When a price breaks a boundary, it may signal that the move is strong enough to continue. When the bands are closer together, it is considered more likely that there will be a price breakout. The bands can be used with any moving average.

Remember, the objective of technical analysis is to find and confirm trading signals using more than one indicator. For example, you may see an M formation, which highlights significant resistance areas. In addition, a short-term moving average may cross the real-time price line above or at the first or second top of that M. Connecting the tops of the M with a trend line, you can project the resistance line going forward.

Using those signals in real time, and based on your trading parameters and time frame, you may determine, for example, a price at which to go short at or near the resistance level. Your buy stop to exit the trade would most likely be placed just above that resistance level or just above the top of the M, since it would represent a significant breakout to the upside should the market trade there. Of, you could go long from a support level, based on a previous U or V pattern, with a profit target at or below the targeted resistance.

At all times, however, you must be watchful for signs of whether the market is likely to be contained by an existing trend or whether it will break out. No trend—up, down, or sideways—will continue forever. At some point and at some price level the dynamics among the buyers and sellers will change, and so will the trend. A true breakout is a move that is sustained by follow-through action, whether continued buying that propels the market higher or selling the pushes it lower. A move that cannot be sustained is known as a fake-out.

PUTTING IT TOGETHER

Exercise 4.4

1. A market that appears to be breaking out to the upside, but buyers retreat at higher price levels. The result is called a:

    A. Breakout.

    B. Fake-out.

    C. Shakeout.

2. Is it easy to see when a breakout is going to be sustained?

    A. Usually

    B. Sometimes

    C. Rarely

3. There are certain times when false breakouts or fake-outs are more common than others.

    A. True

    B. False

4. The best way to determine whether a breakout is real is after the move is over.

    A. True

    B. False

TECHNICAL ANALYSIS IN REVIEW

The purpose of technical analysis is to look for indications, based on current and previous price patterns, of what the market is likely to do next. You cannot rely on one indicator alone, because the market is dynamic and multifaceted. And it's possible for an indicator to be right, but the timing of that indicator may not fit your trading time frame. For example, a trend line may be indicating a "sell" that might not materialize in the market for another day, which will be too late for your day-trading strategy.

RECAP

Exercise 4.5

Figure 4.3 is a chart of Oracle, with 50-day and 200-day moving average lines plotted on the chart. Using this chart, plot the following indicators.

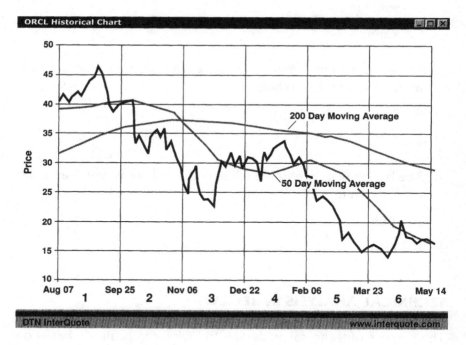

Figure 4.3   ORCL Historical Chart (*Source:* www.interquote.com, DTN Financial Services)

1. Draw a trend line between two significant highs and one between two significant lows. Extend the lines into the future.
   What do the lines show?

2. How do the trend lines relate to the moving average lines?

3. What formations do you perceive on the chart? What does this
   tell you about various market levels?

4. How would you use this information to help you form a "real-
   time opinion" on the market, based on the indicators?

TECHNICAL TERM REVIEW

Exercise 4.6

1. What does a moving average depict?

2. What do trend lines represent?

3. How are moving average envelopes used?

4. What are trend channels useful for?

5. How is using more than one technical indicator helpful?

Coming up . . . The Myths, the Risks, and the Rewards

5

The Myths, the Risks, and the Rewards

As a trader, your goal is to make well-executed trades. This will require your technical analysis and the plotting of each trade to be balanced by your risk and reward.

In this workbook chapter, we'll examine ways in which to control risk, protect your capital, and work toward your goal of making well-executed trades. Whether you're a novice or an experienced professional, your goal is always to make the well-executed trade. You do your analysis; target your entry, exit, and stop points; and then wait for the setup to be confirmed. When all signals are go, you execute the trade—but not until that moment.

That's probably one of the biggest lessons to learn in trading— knowing when to trade and when to wait. If you get in too soon, you could get chopped up by a market that hasn't determined its direction yet. Or if you get in too late, after the move is nearly over, you'll be in danger of chasing the market.

It's all in the timing. I like to trade from the opening until the second hour or so. And I've learned that if I get caught the wrong way in the morning, I'm better off taking a break. If I've been in the pit, it's time to walk back to the office, clear my head, and take care of some business. Inevitably, the market will slow down during the midday hours from roughly 11 A.M. until 1:30 P.M. or so Central time. I used to think that it was because all those Wall Streeters were taking two-martini lunches on the East Coast, which corresponded with those slow times in Chicago. And, of course, the traders in the pit do leave for lunch and come back because it's virtually impossible to stand in that pit all day every day.

From 11 A.M. until 1:30 P.M. or so, I take a break from trading, but my mind is never off the market. I go back over the price action of the morning and see where and how my trading was affected. Did I anticipate a breakout that didn't occur? Did I misjudge the strength of support that ended up being breached? What didn't I see then, I ask myself, and what do I see now?

When 1:30 P.M. Central time rolls around, I'm ready to get back into the market. I sometimes joke that the afternoon session is like *Monday Night Football*. If you get killed on Saturday and Sunday with friendly wagers on the football games, you still have Monday night to get even! (Obviously, there is no comparison between trying to predict which team is going to win a football game and the science and art of trading. But you know what I mean.) Whatever the analogy, the afternoon trading session is my clean slate to go back into the market with a fresh perspective.

The greater your ability to focus your attention on the trade before you—not worrying about what happened on the last trade or anything else that might cloud your concentration—the better chance you'll have of making well-executed trades. The backbone of that solid execution is to control your risk.

First, let's start with a little test of your "risk control" awareness.

CONTROLLING RISK

Exercise 5.1

1. Whatever your profit potential, your loss potential should be the same amount.

    A. True

    B. False

2. The best way to limit your loss is with a stop.

    A. True

    B. False

3. There are *no* circumstances under which a stop should be moved during a trade.

    A. True

    B. False

4. If your losses have mounted, when you see an ideal trade setup you should double the amount of money on that trade to try to cut your losses.

    A. True

    B. False

5. Controlling risk and therefore capital exposure is the primary goal of any trader.

    A. True

    B. False

STOPS

To control risk in your trades, you must use stops every time. No exceptions. The placement of your stop must also be part of your technical analysis. For example, let's say you take a long position in S&Ps at 1301, with a profit objective of 1306, because your technical analysis has indicated a resistance band from 1306.50 to 1307. You place your protective sell stop at 1298.50, just below a key support zone at 1299–1300. Your rationale is that, if the market breached 1299–1300, the downside pressure would increase. Moreover, with a 5-handle profit potential on the way up, your stop is placed at 2.5 handles on the downside. This keeps your risk/reward ratio at 1:2.

The risk/reward rule is that your profit potential must be a minimum of twice what your loss potential is per trade. Put the other way, the amount that you stand to lose must be no more than half of what you stand to gain.

Exercise 5.2

1. If you're long a stock for a day trade at $20 and a profit objective of $22.75, ideally your protective sell stop placement should be at what level?

2. You take a short position in S&Ps at 1305 after the market fails to break through resistance at 1306–1307. You see support at 1299–1300. Where would you place your exit target for a profitable trade?

3. In the preceding example, where would you place your protective buy stop?

TRAILING STOPS

The only time to move a stop during a trade is when you're using a "trailing stop." The objective of a trailing stop is to move your protection up with a continued long position or to move it down with a continued short position. However, the only time to use a trailing stop is with a profitable position. Here's an example:

You establish a long position in a stock at $20 a share. Your profit objective is $22 a share, and your stop loss (protective sell stop placement) is at $18 a share. The stock moves quickly to $22 a share, and buying interest remains strong. Based on the buying momentum, you decide to exit only half your position for a $2-a-share profit, but keep the remainder of your position to exit at $24 a share. In this scenario, you would move your protective stop up to $20 or even $22 a share. At $20 a share, if your stop was hit, you would have a "scratch"—no profit and no loss. At $22, your stop would lock in a profit for the remaining positions.

Trailing stops are always moved in the direction of the trade. You must never lower a sell stop or raise a buy stop *while you're in a trade.*

Exercise 5.3

1. You enter a short position in S&P futures at 1310. You see support at 1304.50–1305 and below that at 1299–1300. You place your exit target at 1305.20. You see key resistance at 1311. Where would you place your protective buy stop?

2. The market moves downward quickly from 1310 to 1306. Selling momentum remains strong as the market is well offered. Instead of covering your entire position, you decide to scale out of half of your position at 1305.20. You decide to cover the rest at 1301, above the next support area. To protect yourself, however, you move your protective buy stop downward. Where would you reposition this trailing stop?

One of the reasons to use a trailing stop is to prevent a winning trade from becoming a loser. For example, let's say you scale out of half of your position at the original target of 1305.20 with the belief that the market will eventually trade to the 1299–1300 support level. But instead, buyers step into the market at 1304.50, the lower end of the first support zone, and the market is quickly bid up to the 1311 level. If your protective buy stop is still at 1311.20 or 1311.40 you'll be stopped out at a higher price for a loser on the remaining portion of the trade. But by moving your protective stop downward—in the direction of the market—you would limit your loss potential and even end up with a profit.

MEASURING RISK

When it comes to taking on risk, there is a point at which every trader has had enough. For experienced, well-capitalized traders, the amount of risk may be far greater than the risk that can be handled by a less experienced trader who is trading smaller positions.

Typically, as your experience and proficiency in making trades increase, you'll increase your trade size. With that, your profit potential and your loss potential also will rise. The key to determining when—and if—to increase your trade size rests in your own self-knowledge and comfort level.

Exercise 5.4

1. Trading 10 futures contracts or 1,000 shares is as easy as trading one contract or 100 shares.

   A. True

   B. False

2. When you trade, you need to disassociate yourself from the money on the line. You need to think of the contracts or shares of stocks that you're buying and selling like you'd think of chips at the casino.

   A. True

   B. False

3. If you're a "buy the dip" trader, you must learn other methods of trading as well.

   A. True

   B. False

4. Your goal as a trader must be to trade as large a position as possible at all times.

   A. True

   B. False

5. If you have a stop in place, there is no way that you'll face more risk than you've determined in advance.

   A. True

   B. False

CAPITALIZATION AND THE WELL-EXECUTED TRADE

When losses mount, there is undeniably something wrong with your trading system: your research, your trading plan, your execution. You must dissect each of your trades to find out exactly what went wrong. Was your stop placement incorrect? Did you risk too much capital? Was your trading plan not backed by technical research—did you trade on a whim?

Capitalization and risk management are inextricably linked. The size of your trade is dictated by the capital you have. To preserve that capital, you must place your stops so that your potential losses are limited. Exit points for a profitable trade must be realistic. Leave the moon shots to NASA. Make solid, well-executed trades.

It bears repeating. Because trading is risky, you can't bet the proverbial farm on it. In other words, start out with only speculative capital, the potential loss of which would not negatively impact your lifestyle. It's not just a disclaimer. It's a rule of survival. If you risk the money you need to pay your mortgage and your bills, put food on the table, and finance your kids' educations, you will severely undermine your trading psychology. If you have to think about every dollar on the line, you will not be able to focus on the trading. Remember, you must think about the trade and *not* the money. If you find yourself in a desperate situation financially, the solution is not to take on any more risk. Even if you believe that you were born to be a trader, you're not in any condition to trade. Take yourself out of the market. Go back to your day job, or get one to raise capital. Keep your mind in the market, but keep your money out of it. You need to get back to the basics.

RISK AND TRADING PSYCHOLOGY

Exercise 5.5

1. When trading, it's good to have a daily profit goal.

    A. True

    B. False

2. Based on my profit goal for the day, I can extrapolate what I stand to make for the month and the year.

    A. True

    B. False

3. Long-term profit targets allow me to look ahead without putting too much daily attention on the money involved.

    A. True

    B. False

4. Trading is a great profession because you only have to work a few hours a day.

    A. True

    B. False

5. I should set a limit for my maximum loss per day.

    A. True

    B. False

YOUR TRADING STYLE

You'll know the signals and indications of your favorite kind of trade, whether it's playing the breakout or selling the rally. And you'll undoubtedly favor either the long or the short side. For day traders the learning curve usually starts out from the long side, but there is a point at which they become comfortable going short. Then it seems that most people like to trade from the short side. There is also a belief out there among traders that the market goes down faster than it goes up. But if you've ever been caught short on a rally, you'll know that the market can skyrocket as quickly as it can plummet.

Exercise 5.6

1. Successful traders typically have one style of trading (i.e., buying the dips, looking for breakouts, etc.).

    A. True

    B. False

2. To trade effectively, you should look to increase the variety of trades that you make.

    A. True

    B. False

3. The key to successful trading is to know when to trade and when not to trade.

   A. True

   B. False

4. Look to buy after the bottom has been put in and look to sell after the top has been made. Do not attempt to pick tops and bottoms.

   A. True

   B. False

5. In trading, the trend is more important than the timing.

   A. True

   B. False

6. Overtrading is not a problem for most traders.

   A. True

   B. False

7. Adding to a position when the market is moving against you is a good idea because doing so will help you to have more favorable entry points on average.

   A. True

   B. False

TRADE EXECUTION

The well-executed trade can be broken down into three steps: ready, aim, and fire.

Ready: This is your initial trade setup from clearing your mind of distractions as you mentally prepare to trade to studying your price charts and reviewing your technical analysis. What's your bias for the day? At what price level would you be a buyer and/or a seller, based on support, resistance, and retracements?

Aim: At this stage, you're watching the market for those setups that you outlined in the first step. Let's say you've identified critical support in a stock or a futures market. The market opens above that level, trades up briefly, then drifts lower. As it nears your support target you tell yourself that it's not going to stay there. You're poised to buy if that happens.

Fire: This is where it all comes together. You've identified the price levels, and you've taken aim as that setup occurs. Now the target is in your sights. You execute a trade at the price you previously identified, with a protective stop and a first profit target.

Exercise 5.7

1. In the beginning, the "ready, aim, fire" steps will be methodical and perhaps a little overly deliberate.

    A. True

    B. False

2. As an experienced trader, you will skip over the "ready" and/or "aim" steps because trading will become second nature to you.

    A. True

    B. False

3. Adhering too strictly to a three-step—ready, aim, fire—process will slow your trading down too much, and you may miss out on too many moves.

    A. True

    B. False

KEEP TRACK OF YOUR TRADES

All traders have their favorite strategies. At the same time, it's imperative that you pick the best strategy for the market conditions at the time. For example, buying the dip and selling the rally will work fine if the market is in a range. The market rises to an established resistance trend line and then breaks, allowing you to sell the rally. The market declines to an established support trend line and then bounces, allowing you to buy the dip.

But what happens when the market trend changes? What will you do when, instead of hitting resistance and breaking, the market keeps going to the upside? If you sold that rally to establish a short position, then you'd be short in a rising market—although one hopes that you would get out at a predetermined loss level. Similarly, if you bought the dip but the market broke through the support line, you'd be long in a falling market. Clearly, your strategy would no longer work.

If you're out of sync with the market it's because you have not yet recognized the "personality" of the market at that time. The quickest way to find out is to look at your losing trades.

It benefits all traders—novices to professionals—to keep a log of their trades. This log should include the time in, time out, whether you were long or short, and the end result.

The times that you've successfully employed your strategy—such as buying the dips/selling the rallies—then you have successfully identified the kind of market you're in. But a rangebound market will eventually break out in one direction or another. Conversely, a trend will end, and a market will become rangebound. When those changes take place, you have to shift your trading strategy as well.

- Your trading log should include every trade you make—win, loss, or scratch.

- Record the time you entered the trade, the size of the trade, the entry point, and whether you were short or long.

- Write down whether you were stopped out or exited the trade deliberately. How long did you stay in the trade? Was the end result a profit or a loss?

- Cumulate data on your trades over time.

- Analyze the results for insights into how you're trading. For example, how long do you typically hold on to a losing trade? How long do you stay in a winning trade?

- What types of trades yield the best results for you?

- Do you favor the long or short side?

These kinds of results can be helpful for many reasons, including seeing where you typically make mistakes. For example, you might discover that you tend to hold on to losing trades far longer than you stay in winning trades. That may mean you don't exit the losing trades fast enough—or perhaps you're exiting the winning trades too soon. Unless you're aware of your own trading patterns over time, you won't know where and how to take corrective action.

Coming up . . . Intraday Dynamics

6

Intraday Dynamics

Each day that you trade, you must prepare yourself. When I talk with traders, I like to draw an analogy to sports. If you were going to run five miles, would you just lace up your shoes and go? Or would you stretch out first? If you were going to play any kind of sport competitively, whether it's a football match or a golf tournament, wouldn't you want to make sure you were in the best form mentally and physically? Trading is no different. Throughout, this workbook has discussed the mental game of trading—the need each day to clear your mind and summon your discipline. Then you're ready for the market preparation.

Perhaps you've studied the charts the night before, and now you're going to review them. Chances are you'll want to see what the overseas markets did, since there is often a carryover effect from the Japanese and European markets to the U.S. markets. What news has been announced overnight? What are the financial TV commentators saying about early-morning actions or comments by stock analysts at the major brokerage firms? Is a major economic report or earnings release scheduled for the preopening or morning hours?

All of this comprises the backdrop for your trading that day. In terms of the "ready, aim, fire" steps discussed in the previous chapter, the preparation is the "ready" component.

We post a preopening "Morning Meeting" on our TeachTrade.com web site, which reviews the premarket activity, gives support/resistance and other important price levels for the day, and also puts the previous day's activity into perspective. This mirrors the preparation we do for our own trading each day; in fact the Morning Meeting posted on the site is a by-product of our own internal "morning meeting" among the traders at the firm.

This workbook chapter goes over some of the more common features and aspects of intraday dynamics. While we often refer to S&P futures, much of what is discussed relates to *any* stock or stock index.

FAIR VALUE

When it comes to trading futures, such as S&P or Nasdaq futures, the premarket activity is often expressed as being above or below "fair value," which is the theoretical premium that the futures market should have over the cash market. Even if you're trading individual stocks, knowing how the stock index futures relate to fair value will give you an early indication of broader market sentiment.

For example, here's an excerpt from the Morning Meeting commentary posted on TeachTrade.com from April 30, 2001: "S&Ps are trading at 1265.50, up 700. . . . We are well above fair value so expect to see follow-through buying on the open."

What this tells you is that the market is out of equilibrium, which will provide some potential opportunities for large players in the market to trade based on the difference between the S&P cash market and the S&P futures market. But that opportunity is usually short-lived. Program trading is triggered, selling futures and buying stocks or vice versa, until the market comes into line with fair value.

For the average trader, however, fair value is probably of most use as a speculative sentiment indicator. In general terms, when futures are below fair value, it's a bearish indicator, and when futures are above fair value it's a bullish sign.

Exercise 6.1

1. Fair value is the mathematical difference, based on interest rates, time to expiration, and the dividends on underlying stocks, between the value of a stock index futures contract and the cash market.

    A. True

    B. False

2. Fair value fluctuates during the day based on market sentiment.

    A. True

    B. False

3. If a stock index futures contract trades significantly above or below fair value during the day, it often sets up program trading aimed at taking advantage of this arbitrage opportunity.

    A. True

    B. False

OPENING RANGE

When trading begins, one of the key things to watch with any stock or index is the opening range. This range is often pivotal for the morning trading session or even the entire trading day. Some traders do use the opening range like a pivot, and they determine whether the market sentiment is bullish or bearish depending on where the market is trading relative to the opening range.

Exercise 6.2

1. As part of your premarket preparation, you identified resistance (based on trend lines) for S&P futures at 1306 to 1307. When

trading begins, the opening range is put in at 1305 to 1307. The market trades higher up to 1308, but can't sustain the upward momentum. It trades lower to the opening range, is unable to move any higher, and then breaks sharply. Given this scenario, how would the opening range factor into your intraday analysis?

2. Continuing this scenario, let's say you have determined a support area at 1299 to 1300. The market trades down to 1299.50, and bounces slightly up to 1301. It then trades between 1299 and 1301 for a half hour. Buyers step in above 1301. At this point, what would you look to do?

3. What would your profit target(s) be on this trade?

4. Let's assume that you did *not* put a position on at 1300. The market rises further to 1303.50. What would you do?

5. If the market was able to cross the opening range and traded through 1308, what setup would you look for? How would you view the opening range at this point?

PRICE LEVELS

As part of your analysis, you have identified key support and resistance levels by using the indicators discussed earlier, such as chart patterns, trend lines, and moving averages. Moreover, you are also looking at the market relative to significant price levels from previous trading sessions.

Exercise 6.3

1. Name some of the significant price levels that you would look for.

2. How would you factor those price levels into your trading strategy?

RETRACEMENTS

One of the significant price levels that are often used as targets for trading are retracements. Simply put, retracements are price levels that reflect a certain percentage of significant moves. For example, in a recent TeachTrade.com market commentary we identified the price level of 1218.60 in S&P futures as an 88 percent retracement of a previous up move from 1215 to 1245.

Retracements that often are used in trading include 25 percent, 33 percent, 50 percent, 75 percent, and 88 percent. In addition, many traders use Fibonacci retracements, named for a twelfth-century Italian mathematician. In the Fibonacci series, two percentages that are commonly used are 61.8 percent and 38.2 percent.

At TeachTrade, we like to watch 88 percent retracements. We find that, over time, the 88 percent retracement level often marks the end of a significant move. At the 88 percent point, the move is likely to run out of steam. It may go farther, making it to 90 percent or even 91 percent retracement. But at that point, the risk of a reversal is usually too great.

Exercise 6.4

1. Retracement levels are found at specific percentage points along the course of a previous market move.

   A. True

   B. False

2. Retracements are based only on upward movements (rallies) and not on downward movements (breaks).

   A. True

   B. False

3. Retracements are important if for no other reason than these points are commonly watched by traders and therefore tend to act like magnets for trading activity.

   A. True

   B. False

4. Assume you are long a stock from $30 a share and the stock is now trading at $35.75. You have previously scaled out of most of your long position, with half sold at $34.50 and a quarter at $35. You kept a quarter position because of continued buying momentum in the stock. However, there is an 88 percent retracement, based on a previous down move, at $36.25. What would you do?

GAPS

Another potential price target is a gap. Gaps are created when the market opens significantly higher or lower than the previous trading day's close. On a chart, the price line literally has a gap. That gap then becomes a target, making one of the most popular day trades: the filling of the gap. Markets fill open gaps about 90 percent of the time, often the day they are created, but commonly within two days. The few times that gaps are not filled usually result in strong, significant moves in the same direction as the gap.

Exercise 6.5

1. On March 12, 2001, S&Ps gapped 12 points lower on rumors in the market of potential Japanese bank failures. The gap was never filled that day. How would you expect S&Ps to have finished the day?

2. A stock gaps at the open on surprise positive news, and trades higher. The gap is not filled that day or in subsequent days. A

few weeks later, however, the stock is under pressure and "left-over" gap is within reach. How would you view that gap?

HOURLY CLOSE

Another factor in intraday dynamics is the hourly close. These inter-vals are watched closely to see where the market ends up in relation to certain key support/resistance levels, retracements, and other price targets. Typically, prices at the close of each 60-minute interval are charted. The easiest way to see this is with candlestick charts (as opposed to the commonly used bar chart). The pattern of the chart then gives an indication of the trend in the market—upward, down-ward, or rangebound. Based on these hourly closes, you may adjust or confirm your trading strategy for the day.

Hourly closes are easily analyzed using a candlestick chart. The price activity for each bar or time interval on the chart is reflected in the formation of the candlestick.

- The candlesticks have thick, vertical bodies that are formed by the difference between the open of that bar or time interval and the close.

- The candles may have "needles" or tops that are spikes above the candlesticks, which trace the high of that time interval.

- The candles may have "tails" or bottoms that are spikes below the candlesticks, which indicate the low of that interval.

Exercise 6.6

1. On a candlestick chart of hourly closes in a given stock or fu-tures contract, the candles show a progressively higher pattern, like steps in a staircase. What does that tell you?

2. A "doji" is a particular kind of candlestick formation that has no body at all, but is all needle and/or tail. How would this formation be made? What might it signal?

3. Your technical analysis indicates that the market needs to get above a particular price for an uptrend to remain intact. The market does trade above this level, which it manages to sustain on an hourly close basis. What does that tell you?

4. Conversely, the market closes below a certain level on an hourly basis. What does this tell you?

Exercise 6.7

The formations discussed in *Workbook* Chapter 4 can appear intraday as well as over a longer period of time. Suppose you have a 30-minute intraday chart of a stock that you're actively analyzing.

1. How would an M formation be made intraday, and what would the significance be?

2. You notice a V formation intraday, with the bottom touching a 10-minute moving average. What does this tell you?

3. A stock has gapped at the open and traded higher. Now it is forming a W above the gap. What does this tell you?

LIMITS

In stock index futures, we note on virtually a daily basis where "limit down" comes in and where the "double limit" would be. This is significant because these limits are the prices at which trading would potentially be halted. Limits are based on percentage moves downward. When those levels are hit, if offers are not made about the limit, trading is halted for 10 minutes.

Exercise 6.8

1. Limits are designed to act as safety valves to prevent a market "meltdown."

   A. True

   B. False

2. The positions of price limits must be taken into consideration in your technical analysis and trading strategy.

   A. True

   B. False

3. If a futures market—such as S&P futures—are locked limit down, what would the S&P cash market tell you?

4. How would you potentially use the cash market activity as part of your trading strategy when the futures limit expires?

FADE TRADE

There are many ways to trade based on intraday dynamics, including following the trend upward or downward with confirming signals. But there are times when you will believe the market is not going to continue a particular move. Significant resistance on the upside will cap an up move, or strong support on the downside will act as a floor. In both cases, you determine that the trend that you have observed is not likely to continue beyond some critical price levels. That's when you might employ the fade trade.

Exercise 6.9

1. Using Nasdaq futures as an example, assume that your technical analysis has identified a key price level at 1920, a price at which

the market has seen a strong two-way trade. The market opens at 1913, well below 1920, and has difficulty reaching this critical zone in the first few minutes. Finally, it struggles above 1920, but can't go higher. What do you assume about the market?

2. If a reversal does develop, what significant price levels would you watch?

3. How would you fade this up move toward 1920 based on the assumptions made thus far?

4.   How would failed retests of old highs and lows factor into a "fade trade" strategy?

STOCK DYNAMICS

Much of our focus thus far has been on the dynamics of stock index futures, particularly the S&P and the Nasdaq, although much of the intraday dynamics discussed here applies to individual stocks. Moreover, the intraday activities of the S&P, Nasdaq, and Dow markets have a direct impact on individual equities.

First, let's start with a simplified look at stock-trading dynamics. Using a Level II screen, you'll be able to see who is dominating the action at the moment—the buyers or the sellers. But you can't trade an individual equity in a vacuum. A variety of intraday dynamics are affecting prices and the perceptions of the buyers and sellers. For example, if buyers believe that the supply of low-priced shares of a particular stock is going to be depleted, they'll step up to buy aggressively. Conversely, if sellers believe that demand for high-priced shares of a particular stock is going to ease, they'll increase the selling pressure.

Now, consider that stock-trading activity in the context of the broader equities market. In fact, equity traders should always know where and how the stock indexes are trading.

• If you trade Nasdaq equities, you will want to have the Nasdaq Composite, an index of all Nasdaq stocks, Nasdaq 100 cash, an index of the top 100 Nasdaq stocks, and Nasdaq futures, based on the Nasdaq 100, on your screen. The Nasdaq 100 futures are considered one of the best indicators of stock price activity for individual Nasdaq 100 stocks.

- In addition, you may want to monitor other major indexes, such as the Dow and the S&P 500.

- You may also want to track other indexes, such as Semiconductors (SOX), which is often seen as a proxy for movements in the Nasdaq, and/or the Banking index (BKX), which may be moving in concert with the S&Ps.

- On a Level II screen, you'll focus on current bids and offers, as well as time and sales. The bids and offers show you what players are active in a stock and at what price. The time and sales data will show you what prices have traded and in what quantity. If the current price is lower than the previous transaction, it is often displayed in red. If the price is higher, it is displayed in green.

Whatever you trade, you must remember that the market is dynamic—not static. You can't pick your price targets in the morning based on the previous day's activity, and trade in a vacuum. The market is constantly moving (even when it's stuck in a range), moving toward support and resistance, testing and retesting old lows and highs, making new intraday highs and lows, or failing at these previous levels.

Each of these events must be added to your real-time analysis of the market. Think of it as a map that's laid out one step at a time. You can't just assume the path will be a straight line. It's the same with the market. At any given time the market may be acting and/or reacting to certain dynamics in the marketplace. You may not be aware of every nuance, news announcement, and/or rumor, but if you study the charts in real time and engage in ongoing analysis, you'll see the impact of those events on the market.

Exercise 6.10

1. Once the trend is set for the day—bullish or bearish—it rarely changes intraday.

    A. True

    B. False

2. It's possible to have a short-term negative trend, but a longer-term positive or neutral trend.

    A. True

    B. False

3. Two traders can conceivably make money in the same market from opposite ends of key price levels.

    A. True

    B. False

4. You can be right about the market trend but still have a losing trade.

    A. True

    B. False

Coming up . . . Trading the Nasdaq

7

Trading the Nasdaq

Oh, the Nasdaq. . . .

So much has been written about the rocket-rise of the Nasdaq in 1999, and then the "crash and burn" of 2000 and the weakness in the first months of 2001. But if we look at very recent history—in fact, the days in which this workbook was being completed—it reveals a very interesting image of this market. Here are excerpts of the TeachTrade.com Morning Meeting commentary on the Nasdaq from three days in May 2001.

May 14, 2001: Nasdaq [futures] are trading down 500 [points] at 1829.50. For today, we have support between 1820 and 1805. Within this zone is Friday's low of 1816. If we get below here, look for a move to 1750. Along the way, 1795 to 1790 is support, and below that 1775 to 1765 is support. Limit-down today comes in at 1749.50. . . .

May 22, 2001: Nasdaq is trading up 21 at 2073. As we have been commenting for some time, and we stated yesterday, once this market went to 2000 we did not think it would stop on the upside. . . . For today, we have support between 2040 and 2029. Under that, look for 2010. We have key support between 2015 and 2005. Only a settlement below 2000 will put this rally into question. . . .

May 30, 2001: Nasdaq is trading down 33 at 1823.50. SUNW [Sun Microsystems] is the issue at hand, as we are now starting the quarterly earnings warnings season. SUNW came out at 3:10 P.M. Central yesterday with some negative news in terms of lowered expectations and revenue projections for the up-coming quarter. This led to a settlement in the futures at 17 points below the cash settle. The further erosion this morning certainly leads one to think that the market may be betting on more companies issuing similar warnings shortly. Also worth noting, we are now about 10 percent off our highs made five trading sessions ago—a very quick decline. . . .

The kind of volatility and uncertainty just described is a hallmark of the Nasdaq index itself and of many of the individual stocks within the Nasdaq. This is the challenge and the opportunity of trad-ing highly volatile markets such as the Nasdaq.

As we explore the dynamics of this unique market, let's start with the basic terminology.

The Nasdaq 100 is an index of the largest and most active nonfi-nancial domestic and international issues listed on the Nasdaq, based on market capitalization.

NASDAQ futures are based on the value of the Nasdaq 100 cash index.

The Nasdaq Composite is comprised of all Nasdaq domestic and non-U.S.-based common stocks listed on this exchange.

Nasdaq is a market-value–weighted index, meaning that each company affects the index in proportion to its value (total shares outstanding multiplied by the most recent sale price). Thus the bigger stocks throw their weight around in the Nasdaq with far more impact than the smaller companies. As of April 25, 2001, the largest stocks in the Nasdaq 100 were: Microsoft (MSFT), Intel (INTC), Qualcomm (QCOM), Cisco Systems (CSCO), and Oracle (ORCL).

Exercise 7.1

1. What makes the Nasdaq so volatile are the gyrations of the largest stocks in the index.

   A. True

   B. False

2. The Nasdaq Composite ended 1999 with a gain of:

   A. 74.6 percent

   B. 56.8 percent

   C. 85.6 percent

   D. 113.5 percent

3. The Nasdaq Composite ended 2000 with a loss of:

   A. 39.3 percent

   B. 42.7 percent

   C. 22.5 percent

4. What led to the decline in Nasdaq in 2000 and early 2001?

5. The "spike up/spike down" pattern in the Nasdaq in 1999 and 2000 would have what psychological and technical impacts in 2001 and going forward?

WATCHING THE STOCKS

Because Nasdaq is a weighted index (and the largest-capitalization stocks have the most influence on the index) it is vital that a Nasdaq futures trader watch the major stocks. Conversely, if you're trading individual Nasdaq stocks, then the movement of the index itself is a proxy and potential leading indicator for what might happen in the larger issues.

Starting with Nasdaq futures (based on the value of the Nasdaq 100), be aware of the movement of the top five holdings. At this writing, these five stocks are Microsoft, Intel, Qualcomm, Cisco, and Oracle. Together, these five stocks comprise more than 25 percent of the entire index's capitalization.

Here's a simple way to find out the composition and relative weighting of the top stocks in the Nasdaq 100:

1. Go to the Nasdaq.com web site at www.nasdaq.com.

2. Click on Market Activity to view the market indexes.

3. Select Nasdaq 100 from the menu.

4. Select View List of Securities.

5. Scroll down to find the list of 100 stocks in the Nasdaq 100 (listed alphabetically). The relative weighting of each stock is also given.

Exercise 7.2

1. Suppose one of the "big five" stocks in the Nasdaq announces after the stock market close that it has lowered revenue growth expectations. What would you expect to be the impact on the Nasdaq futures when trading resumes the next day?

2. Conversely, one of the "big five" has an earnings surprise, also released after the stock market close. What would you expect to be the impact on Nasdaq the next morning?

There are times, however, when the market will seemingly shrug off news from a major Nasdaq stock. This may be because the news has already been factored into the market, or there is a strong underlying bullish or bearish trend that counters the news from one stock. And, of course, the market—any market—is being influenced by a variety of factors at any given time. Thus, Nasdaq traders must also watch the second tier of stocks.

These second tiers—as the name implies—are the next several stocks after the big five in terms of market weighting. Often, as we've seen recently, these second tiers may be a closer proxy for the Nasdaq market sentiment—particularly if one or more of the big five is being unduly influenced by news (positive or negative) related to that one company.

To underscore the importance of the stock–stock index correlation, keep in mind that we spend as much time analyzing the top 30 stocks in the Nasdaq 100 as we do the index futures themselves! What we're looking for is a significant movement in one or more of these key stocks as an indication of what might happen in the broader index.

NASDAQ PROXIES

There are other benchmarks that act as proxies for the overall behavior of the Nasdaq index.

- *Semiconductors index (SOX):* Traded on the Philadelphia Stock Exchange, this price-weighted index is composed of 16 U.S. companies primarily involved in the design, distribution, manufacture, and sale of semiconductors.

- *PHLX/The Street.com Internet Sector (DOT):* Also traded on the Philadelphia Stock Exchange, this is an equal-dollar-weighted index composed of 24 leading companies involved in Internet commerce, service, and software.

- *Nasdaq Biotechnology index (IXBT):* This index contains companies primarily engaged in using biomedical research.

- *Amex Networking index (NWX):* This is an index of networking stocks.

LISTENING TO THE MARKET

Exercise 7.3

1. The SOX index is up 2.2 percent on the day. What does that po-
    tentially tell you about Nasdaq and/or individual stocks you
    might be trading?

2. The Nasdaq 100 is trading up marginally even though one of the
    big five is off on company-specific news. The SOX is hovering
    between unchanged and slightly positive. What else should you
    be watching for clues to the Nasdaq behavior and/or sentiment?

3. IBM obviously trades on the New York Stock Exchange, and not
    the Nasdaq. Therefore, what happens in IBM will have no im-
    pact on the Nasdaq.

    A. True

    B. False

4. You notice that Microsoft—the biggest stock in the Nasdaq 100
    in terms of market weighting—has just closed above its 200-day
    moving average for the first time in months. What impact would
    that have on the Nasdaq?

DEALING WITH VOLATILITY

With a market like the Nasdaq, a little perspective goes a long way.
For example, let's take a look at the TeachTrade.com "Week in Review" commentary for the week ended May 26, 2001. Earlier in the
week, we had seen continued strength in the stock index futures, followed by profit taking on Thursday and Friday of that week. Here's
how Brad Sullivan of TeachTrade put it all in perspective:

> On Monday morning, it appeared as though we were off to the
> races, as S&P futures (SPM) printed a new recent high at 1319,

the Nasdaq futures (NDM) participated in a large rally, settling at 2052, and the DJIA was at 11,350. But the momentum subsided, and by the end of the week the DJIA settled just above 11,000 and the NDM failed to hold 2,000, closing up only about 2 percent on the week. Finally, the SPM settled off about 1.4 percent.

The question now becomes was this just a necessary breather in a bull market, or was it something more? The facts are this: The SPX (S&P cash) failed 1 point short of its 50 percent retracement from the all-time high to the spring 2001 lows. The NDX has not retraced even 25 percent of the down move from the March 2000 highs.

I think the failure to capture and hold above key levels (NDM 2000) is somewhat disappointing. However, in the larger scheme this level may be traded around for some period before the market picks a direction.

This kind of scenario is not unexpected given the uncertainty of the marketplace following momentous moves in 1999 and 2000, as well as the volatility of the Nasdaq marketplace itself. Once again, consider the kind of stocks that are in this index—technology, growth-oriented, and still with comparatively high P/E ratios. Comprised of these kind of stocks, it's no wonder that Nasdaq can undergo some dramatic gyrations.

This underlying volatility will affect your trading strategy. Because of their generally volatile nature, Nasdaq futures require traders to use wider stops than they normally would. Our professional traders, for example, use fairly wide stops as a rule in Nasdaq futures. In general, you might consider stops that take into account a 1.25 percent to 3 percent move.

Exercise 7.4

1. Your normal stop placement is not working in your Nasdaq trades. You notice that, given the market volatility, you are getting stopped out on the majority of your trades. How can you prevent this?

2. How will this decision affect your overall risk?

3. What should you do to maintain your risk level?

AIR BALLS

Another phenomenon that we see in volatile markets such as the Nasdaq, particularly when conditions are volatile and movements are fast, is the "air ball." In basketball, when a player shoots for the hoop but misses completely—no backboard, no rim, no net—it's called an air ball. From the minute the ball leaves a player's hands until it hits the floor it doesn't touch anything but air.

This kind of action can happen frequently in the Nasdaq, where an "air ball" can sometimes cover 20 handles—or even more. What happens then is there is nothing between one price and another but "air"—or, more precisely, massive acceleration to the upside or the downside.

Exercise 7.5

1. On February 13, 2001, Nasdaq futures were trading at 2312 before a final hour sell-off that took the market down to 2212. Describe that phenomenon.

What causes air balls (which are sometimes called "air pockets")? Perhaps there is speculation about an event or a rumor that circulates that sends a shiver of panic through the market. Short positions are dumped. Long positions are exited quickly. Whatever the reason, it's apparent that air balls—sudden, rapid, and sometimes unexplained events—are going to happen, especially in a dramatically volatile market like the Nasdaq.

EXTENSIONS

Another feature of a volatile market such as the Nasdaq is an "extension," which is simply a percentage change from various moving averages. For example, let's say the 20-day moving average in the Nasdaq is at 2500. If the current price is 2650, that would be a 6 percent upside extension. Plotting these extensions on a graph, you can analyze these correlations to see when—and where—the market is abnormally extended.

Typically what we find is that a bounce or a reversal is more likely to happen when the Nasdaq trades at more than a 12 percent extension from the 20-day moving average. But in recent history, given the dramatic moves in the Nasdaq, we have seen some monumental extensions. For example, at its high in March 2000 the Nasdaq Composite was about 58 percent above its 200-day moving average, an abnormally wide extension to the upside. The biggest reading on the downside was at the low of 2001 when the index was 63 percent below its 200-day moving average.

Exercise 7.6

1. Suppose Nasdaq futures have extended 22 percent above the 20-day moving average. How do you view the potential for a further upside move?

2. Suppose Nasdaq futures are 6 percent below the 20-day moving average. What impact would this have on a downside move?

3. Suppose Nasdaq futures have extended 27 percent above the 20-day moving average. You decide to exit a long position. Would you get short immediately?

NASDAQ CHECKLIST

It is important for traders of Nasdaq stocks and Nasdaq futures to look for correlations between the two. To do this effectively, you must be able to watch, analyze, and synthesize information from a variety of sources. Here are suggestions of what you should track daily and intraday:

- Keep the top five Nasdaq stocks on your screen. Watch for activity at support and resistance levels, retracements, and so forth in these stocks. Keep an ear tuned to the financial news for announcements or comments regarding these stocks—for example, if one of the big five is suddenly upgraded or downgraded by an analyst, or makes a comment about earnings.

- Watch the second-tier stocks. While their weightings in the Nasdaq 100 are not as large as those of the big five, they do cast their share of influence over the market. It's particularly important to watch the second tier when the market is discounting (meaning ignoring) the movement in the big five.

- Be on the alert for news in other technology stocks, even if they aren't Nasdaq issues.

- Given the dominance of technology on the Nasdaq, watch for movements in the subindexes, such as the SOX (Semiconductors) and DOT (Internet), mentioned earlier in this chapter. The SOX is often a proxy for the Nasdaq. Many times, if we see a rally in the SOX, we can expect the Nasdaq to turn around, and when the SOX breaks the Nasdaq is often soon to follow.

- If you're trading Nasdaq stocks, your radar screen will look much the same as a Nasdaq futures trader's screen. You'll be tracking the movements of the Nasdaq 100 futures and the subindexes. In addition, keep an eye on similar stocks. For example, if you're trading a networking stock, look at other companies in that sector. If a rally or a sell-off in one stock is not company-specific but rather sector-related, you will want to know that as soon as possible.

- Read the headlines. There are many online news sources that you can scroll through during the day. If you can configure your screen to have scrolling headlines, then do so.

SAMPLE NASDAQ TRADE

On the morning of May 9, 2001, Nasdaq futures were trading limit down, off 42 at 1950, after a lower session overnight on the Chicago

Mercantile Exchange's Globex electronic trading platform. That was setting the stage for a weaker opening. If the market fell further, double limit down would come in at 1857.50.

We saw support below the first limit at 1890 to 1885. Below that, support was found at 1875 to 1865. Underneath the double limit, we had strong support between 1850 and 1835. On the upside, we saw resistance at 1900 to 1910, and above that at 1925 to 1935.

When trading began, Nasdaq futures gapped lower to 1900.50. There was little volatility in the trading that morning. In fact, the market was making lower highs and higher lows.

Exercise 7.7

1. What is the setup thus far?

2. What is the tone of the market at this point?

3. What is the significance of this kind of activity?

4. With a triangle pattern, what would you project?

The top of the triangle was a resistance line around 1884. The market moved above it, with good upward momentum. At that point we went long Nasdaq futures. Our exit target was 1895, which was the previous high from the start of the triangle pattern.

The trade was executed successfully. We exited at 1895 some 15 minutes after the position was first put on.

This trade example shows the use of the kind of technical analysis and trade planning that we've discussed through the book. The setup is bearish with a gap at the open. But the early-morning trading formed a triangle or wedge pattern. Plotting the resistance and support lines (which form the triangle), we could see the key areas that the market had to cross in order to break out in one direction or the other.

No one learns to trade just from a book. While certain principles and concepts can be outlined and explained, the real education occurs in the market. That's why at TeachTrade.com we believe that most people face a one-year learning curve during which their experience and proficiency build. In reality, however, the learning curve never ends. The market is always your best teacher as you examine the trades that you make and the end result, whether it's a profit or a loss.

Over the years, I've been asked to share my "secret" to successful trading. There is no magic formula or never-fail system. Trading requires two important things—dedication and discipline.

To succeed, trading must be your passion. You must be willing to give what is necessary in terms of time, talent, and patience. You know that in your first year, you should not look to make any money beyond just covering your costs. *Trading is not a "get rich quick" proposition.*

Discipline goes without saying. You must have the discipline to follow your trading plan and never to break the basic rules, such as by trading without stops, chasing the market, or taking on too much risk for your capitalization. Discipline is what will help you control your emotions, cut your losses quickly, and move on to the next trade.

I can explain these concepts and describe the emotions you'll feel and the challenges you'll face. But until you're there—in the market—you won't really know what to expect of the market or of yourself.

ANSWERS

1

Answers to The Mental Game

Exercise 1.1

Psychological profile scoring:

80 and Above

Your score indicates that your ideas of trading may be inconsistent with the day-to-day rigors of this business. Perhaps you should reevaluate your ideas about day trading and your motivation. This can be done through a systematic elimination process of your negative misconceptions about trading. Go back to the questions and take another look.

60–80

Your score indicates you may have a more long-term business outlook for trading. In fact, if you choose to trade, perhaps you should consider developing a style suited toward duration trades of three to eight weeks.

40–60

Your score indicates you may have an ideal psychological makeup to be a short-term or day trader. You appear to have an aggressive personality that can seemingly handle the emotional swings of this business.

20–40

Your score indicates that you may actually be too short-term in your time horizon, which may lead to indecisiveness in your decision making. You may need to develop an effective system of trading that you believe in.

0–20

Your score indicates you may be too extreme for trading. You may need to work on analysis and outlook before succeeding as a trader. This can be done through visualization, goal setting, and achievement plans.

Exercise 1.2

1. *False.* When you trade, your primary motivation is to make well-executed trades based on technical research. While there is no denying that traders want to make money—just like any entrepreneur—it cannot be the motivating factor. If it is, then the desire—or the need—to make money will cloud your judgment. If you focus only on the money, you're at risk for trading too much or when conditions are not conducive to making a good trade, such as when the market does not have a clear direction. But if your goal is a well-executed trade, you will have a better chance of success and, therefore, of making a profit.

2. *False.* The number one quality for all traders is discipline. Without discipline, it will be very difficult, if not impossible, for you to be successful as a trader. Discipline will allow you to focus objectively on your trading plan without letting your emotions— especially those two big demons, greed and fear—get in the way. The ability to take on and handle a certain amount of risk is certainly a prerequisite. But more important is the discipline to assess your risk and to trade accordingly.

3. *True.* Trading is not for everyone. Even if you have enjoyed tremendous financial success in another profession, it's no guarantee that you'll make it as a trader. For some people the gyra-

tions of the market and the knowledge that they will have losses are too much. Others are not disciplined enough to stick with a trading plan. Losses eat away at their capital until they take on an all-or-nothing attitude. When the market gets crazy, you can't become immobilized like the proverbial deer in the headlights. At the same time, you can't become a loose cannon, firing off trades without thinking.

4. *False.* It's true that many traders do have a healthy quantity of self-confidence. There is a certain amount of self-assuredness that you need to trade. You must be able to make a decision and stick with it. But don't confuse confidence with ego. Confidence comes when you can devise a trading plan and execute according to that plan. Confidence comes from knowing you can cut your losses and move on to the next trade, and let your profits run to a predetermined exit point. Ego, however, deludes you into believing that you have the market all figured out or that you can outsmart the market. When you trade you have to lose your ego. You need to silence your ego in order to listen to the market and to follow what your technical analysis is telling you.

5. *True.* In trading, there is no wishing, hoping, or praying for a particular outcome in the market. There are only the hard, cold facts of the prices on the screen. If you put on a position and the market goes against you, there is no point hoping it will turn around. If you wait, praying for some market miracle to bail you out of a losing position, you run the risk of facing an even larger loss. Rather, your trades must be based on technical analysis. Before you place a trade, you must know not only your entry point, but where you'll exit for a profit, and where you will place a stop to get out of a losing trade at a predetermined loss level.

6. *False.* Your main concern as a trader is to limit your losses. Your profits will take care of themselves. If you focus on keeping your losses small—particularly as a beginning trader—you will preserve your capital. This will also help you to develop the discipline of exiting losing positions quickly and efficiently. At the

same time, you do need to let your profits run to the exit price that is indicated by your technical analysis. At the risk of over-simplifying, remember the goal of trading is to buy low, sell high. To accomplish that, you must exit the losers quickly before you end up buying high and selling low.

7. *False.* As a trader, you need to know when to trade and when to wait. There will be times when your trading system or strategy will have a clear signal to buy or sell. But if the market lacks a clear direction or your system has not generated a trade with low risk and a relatively high potential for success, then it's usually better to wait. Being on the sidelines doesn't mean that your mind is out of the market, though. Keep looking for opportunities and watching your indicators, and determine when the conditions are the most favorable for making a trade. By the same token, it's not rational to expect to sit at the computer screen from opening bell to closing bell. You need to take a break during the day. Find the most advantageous times for you and your system. Maybe you want to trade the first 90 minutes. Or perhaps you want to watch the first 30 minutes and then trade the next hour or two after a trend has been established. Whatever your market, whatever your style, know that there will be optimal times for you to trade and others when you must take a break, clear your head, and go back to studying the charts.

8. *True.* My grandfather used to tell me that it was hard to learn a lesson unless it cost you something. When I was a kid and touched a hot stove (even though I had been told a million times not to), feeling that burn for a moment drove that lesson home. By the same token, a trader may know something intellectually—such as always trade with stops, never trade by your gut instinct alone, and don't add to a losing position when the market is going against you. But until you suffer from that mistake, you won't really learn that lesson. When you have a losing trade, you know there was something wrong with your trade setup, execution, or technical analysis. Dissect each losing trade. See what went wrong, and then figure out what you

should have done differently. In that way, you can discover and correct your mistakes before they take you out of the market.

9. *False.* A string of losses is a signal to slow down, not to speed up. In fact, we suggest that after three losing trades in a row, it's important to take a break, reevaluate your trade setup, and then begin again. That break also allows you to quickly regain your composure (if necessary), instead of letting emotions creep in. It's hard not to feel anger—whether it's aimed at yourself or at the market in general—when you have a string of losses. But this anger and other volatile emotions are really self-defeating. Take a break, clear your head, and become even more focused. Trade smaller and more deliberately. Look for low-risk trades to increase your chances of turning a profit.

10. *False.* There is no holy grail of trading. There is no one indicator or methodology that will work every time. Rather, you must be observant, dedicated, disciplined, and flexible in order to:

   • Analyze market conditions.

   • Pinpoint strategic price levels, including support, resistance, and retracement levels.

   • Plot your trading execution, and execute according to plan.

   • Stick with your plan, regardless of the conclusion.

Exercise 1.3

1. Of course, it's *all of the above.* When you are faced with a losing streak, you must give yourself a break—literally. When you've cut your losses and exited all positions, leave the computer. Clear your head. Take a walk. Get away from the screen. It won't do you any good to obsess right now over what you could have done. Then, go back to your charts. Reexamine what elements determine your trade setups. Did you miss a signal? Or was there an unforeseen event? Did you remember to trade with a

stop? When you reenter the market, cut down your position size. Be very deliberate in your trading. Don't worry about missing a move now. Your priority is to turn a profit—no matter how small—to get your confidence and your rhythm back.

2. *False.* Stops are supposed to take you out of the market at a pre-determined loss level. Not trading with stops is like driving a race car without brakes. It's true that your stops may be too tight for the market volatility (as we'll discuss), but you must place your stops based on your trading style and technical analysis.

3. *False.* Trading involves losses. Period. In fact, you may experience more losing trades than winners, especially in the beginning. But if you cut your losses quickly and let your profits run, you can still have a net profit on your trading.

4. *True.* Too many traders—novices and the more experienced alike—find it difficult to get out of a losing trade. It's as if they can't believe what they see. The market *has* to turn around, they tell themselves. So instead of getting out with a stop, they cancel or move their stop to another level based on the belief that the market will turn around. The danger is that the market will go even further against you, and what was a manageable loss now becomes unmanageable. Here's a joke around our office that illustrates this point: "What's the best way to turn a day trader into a position trader? Answer: Have the market move against him. Then he'll hang on and on and on and on."

Exercise 1.4

1. B. *Sometimes.* This is a tricky one. There are times when you will withdraw some of your profits, either for living expenses or potentially to reward yourself. But a better strategy would be to take the majority of what you withdraw and put it in a safe, long-term investment portfolio. Further, you must never deplete your trading capital by losses or withdrawals from your trading account. One common mistake that young traders, in particular,

make when the market is going their way is that they are quick to spend their profits. First comes the Rolex, and then the Ferrari, and then the vacation house. Eventually the market gets quiet or stops trending in one direction. That's when the experienced traders get to work and the newcomers can't trade the way they used to. Then you can have the Rolex, the Ferrari, the vacation house all at half price. (At the Chicago Mercantile Exchange there was a certain young trader—not to be named—who we used to say wore half his profits on his wrist and drove the other half around town.)

2. C. *Maybe.* Increasing trade size is a step that traders should aim for, but not make too soon. Obviously, trading larger will increase your profit potential, but also your loss potential. The most important thing to remember is not to expose too much of your capital on each trade. Nor should you ever trade such a large position that you can't mentally or emotionally separate the money on the line from the need to make a well-executed trade.

2

Answers to Getting Started

Exercise 2.1

1. *False.* When you enter your stock order electronically, you are transmitting it via the Internet to your broker. Your broker, in turn, must decide how that order is executed. Online trading does expedite getting your order to your broker, but in most cases it still must be routed for execution in one of several different ways.

2. *False.* (But if only that were true!) In trading, slippage is a fact of life. Slippage is the difference between the price you see on a screen and the price at which your trade is executed. The differential can be substantial. This is particularly true in fast-moving markets. In addition, it may be difficult to get a desired price for the quantity of shares or contracts you're trading. You can try to get around this by using price orders, which must be filled at a specified price. But then you run the risk of not getting filled at all because the market has moved beyond your specified prices.

3. *True.* Your broker generally has a choice of ways for your trade to be executed. The Securities and Exchange Commission's web

site (www.sec.gov) offers an in-depth explanation of the various options in trade execution. They are, in summary:

- For stocks listed on the New York Stock Exchange, for example, your broker may direct the order to that exchange, to a regional exchange, or to a "third market maker." A third market maker is a firm that buys or sells stocks listed on an exchange at publicly quoted prices. Some regional exchanges or third market makers will pay your broker for routing your orders to them, sometimes paying $0.01 per share for your order. This is called "payment for order flow."

- Stocks traded on the Nasdaq may be sent to a NASDAQ market maker. Many of these market makers also pay for order flow.

- Your broker may also route your order to an electronic communications network (ECN), an electronic marketplace in which buys and sells are automatically matched at specific prices.

- The brokerage firm may fill your order internally, selling stock to you from its own inventory of shares or buying your stock for its inventory. In this way, the brokerage has the opportunity to make money on the spread, which is the difference between the purchase price and the sale price of a stock.

4. *True.* According to the SEC, your broker has a duty to seek the best execution possible by evaluating all the options—including competing markets, market makers, and ECNs. "The opportunity for 'price improvement'—which is the opportunity, but not the guarantee, for an order to be executed at a better price than what is currently quoted publicly—is an important factor a broker should consider in executing its customers' orders," the SEC notes.

5. *False.* Electronic communications networks (ECNs) compete with the traditional exchanges for stock execution. Approved by market regulators, ECNs are allowed to engage in trading directly between buyers and sellers in an electronic format.

6. *True.* Direct access does give you, the trader, the choice of where and how your order is executed. While direct access may

help you avoid time delay and reduce slippage on your orders, it is not for the beginner. Rather, once you become comfortable with trading, you may then opt for direct access. In addition to having more control over your trades with direct access, you also have more responsibility for them.

7. *False.* In futures, orders can be executed in only one place: at an exchange. And it would be illegal for your broker to take the other side of your futures trade. Let's use the example of S&P and Nasdaq futures, which trade at the Chicago Mercantile Exchange. During the day, S&P and Nasdaq "major contracts"—the full-scale futures contracts—trade only in the pit via open outcry. Thus, if you have orders for majors to be executed, your order will be transmitted either by phone or electronically to the trading desk at the Chicago Merc. If you're trading the scaled-down S&P or Nasdaq mini contracts—one-fifth the size of the majors—your order will be entered by your broker on the Globex system. Globex is the Merc's electronic trading platform, which automatically matches buys and sells based on price and size.

Exercise 2.2

1. D. *All of the above.* Paper trading can help you to practice picking entry and exit points, stop placement, and watching market activity.

2. *False.* The only way that paper trading is effective is if you write down and examine every trade that you identify—including the ones that you later deem to be "dumb mistakes" or false starts. When you're trading real-time, you won't have the opportunity to gloss over a misjudgment. If it results in a loss, you'll have to take it.

3. *False.* We'd never go so far as to say paper trading or online demos are worthless. As previously noted, paper trading can provide practice for order execution. The only drawback, however, is that it cannot replicate the emotional and psychological

aspects of trading. When you're paper trading, for example, you tend to focus on the entry point and the exit point, and whether your stop is touched. In real trading, emotions can accompany every tick (although you must try to control your emotions so that they don't cloud your decision making). You may feel agony when the market moves a tick against you, or euphoria when it moves a tick in your direction. Paper trading cannot prepare you for those highs and lows.

4. *False.* You can open a brokerage account to trade futures for as little as $5,000. In fact, for $5,000 some futures brokers would allow you to trade either one S&P e-mini contract (the scaled-down version of the S&P major contract) or two S&P e-minis intraday. An account at a stock brokerage firm can be opened for as little as $1,000. Ask your brokerage what minimum balances apply to the kind of activity (investing, short-term trading, active day trading) you want to pursue. Find out what fees (including account maintenance) might apply to your account size. Also remember when you're trading never to risk capital that you can't afford to lose. Put another way, remember that you should use only speculative capital, the loss of which won't affect your lifestyle or livelihood.

5. *True.* It is fairly easy to qualify for a margin account for stock trades, provided that you have a minimum balance that meets your brokerage's criteria. For most retail investors, the margin is 2 to 1. Thus, if you want to buy 100 shares of a $50 stock, you can either pay $5,000 outright or pay $2,500 up front and borrow the rest from the brokerage firm by trading on margin. Active professional traders may qualify for higher margin rates, such as 6 to 1 or as high as 10 to 1.

6. *False.* Using the preceding example, if you buy 100 shares of a $50 stock on margin (putting up $2,500 and using margin for the remainder) your losses will be predicated on the full $5,000 value. The brokerage firm will not absorb any portion of the losses.

Exercise 2.3

1. B. *Market order.* In this scenario, you would probably want to enter a market order, which would be executed at the prevailing price immediately. There may be some slippage, meaning the price at which you are filled would be different than the price you saw on your screen due to market conditions. (In a fast-moving market the differential would, in general, be wider than normal.) With a price order, you may miss the chance to get in the market if the specified price were too low for a buy or too high for a sell. A limit order might be used if you wanted to get in the market, but not any higher or lower than a specific level.

2. B. *Price order.* You would enter price orders to be a seller at 1308 and a buyer at 1300. You might mark the price order "OB" ("or better"), requesting that the broker buy at or below 1300 and sell at 1308 or higher if possible.

3. C. *Price order.* You would enter a market if touched (MIT) order for 1301.50. By entering MIT you are instructing your broker to buy if the 1301.50 level is touched and then becomes the low of the day. Thus, even if you couldn't get filled at 1301.50, your order would be filled at the nearest possible price after the 1301.50 level was touched.

4. Ideally, you would have a price order MIT for your upside objective at 1304. Your stop at 1296 would be entered as a sell stop. The orders would be entered "OCO"—order-cancels-other (or one-cancels-other). This means that if the market reaches your upside objective of 1304, the stop at 1296 would be canceled. Conversely, if the market falls and you're stopped out at 1296, the 1304 price order would be canceled.

Exercise 2.4

1. *True.* Real-time information is a definite advantage in the marketplace for active traders. Delayed quotes are useful only to

buy-and-hold investors for whom a 20-minute delay is immaterial. If you are trading, you must know where the market is in real time. Real-time information, however, does not guarantee you any success.

2. *False.* If you're trading, you must know as much as possible about the sector or market that you're trading (such as semiconductor stocks or the Nasdaq). Information on other markets may be insightful for a broader picture, but you can't expect to keep track of multiple markets in real time. Too much information can create an overload that not only distracts you, but hinders your decision-making process. Focus on the information that is most germane to your market. For example, if you're trading Nasdaq futures, you'll want to watch the performance of the other stock indexes (the S&Ps and the Dow) as well as the largest Nasdaq stocks that make up the Nasdaq 100.

3

Answers to Technical Analysis 101

Exercise 3.1

1. One of the standout features of this chart is the mountain peak at the left of the chart. On this chart, the first "peak" is higher than subsequent moves.

2. The pre-October peak is followed by a decline (mid-October 2000) and then a succession of peaks and valleys thereafter. Each of these peaks has a symmetry to it, up one side and down the other. Most importantly, however, the first peak remains the "highest high" that the market makes. All the subsequent highs are below the first area—a classic downtrend. There are several examples of symmetry such as the rise from late October to the peak plateau in early November to the decline in mid-November. This formation on the chart resembles a flat-topped mesa instead of the usual mountain peak.

Exercise 3.2

1. *False.* A short-term trader may hold a trade for several days, but he or she would likely refer to both daily and intraday charts.

Remember, charts of any time frame can tell you something about the prevailing trends for that time period. A short-term trader may use daily charts to see the patterns (and indicators) covering several days. But intraday charts would also be useful in helping to view the very short-term dynamics, analyzing intraday support and resistance, and examining what key price levels are targeted on both daily and intraday charts.

2. *False.* A day trader would use intraday charts to plot and track a position. But just as with the short-term trader in the preceeding question, using a different time perspective offers another view of the market dynamics.

Exercise 3.3

1. *False.* The problem with so-called mental stops is that it is far too tempting to change your mind when the market moves against you. Instead of getting out at, say, $20.25, you convince yourself that the market is going to turn around at any moment, so you'll wait until $20 . . . then $19.90 . . . $19.80. . . . While you wait, your losses mount.

2. *False.* While it's true that stops *can* get you out of the market just before the market turns around, there is far greater danger in trading without stops or with stops that are placed too far away to be useful in protecting you from loss. If you are consistently stopped out of the market, you may want to widen your stop placement. However (as we'll discuss later in the chapter on Nasdaq trading), if you widen your stop placement you must also cut down your trade size so that your overall risk exposure is not increased.

3. *True.* One example is the "stop reversal." This is used to exit a position and to initiate another position. For example, you may see 2012 in Nasdaq futures as a pivotal area, below which you want to be short and above which you would be long. Trading

from the short side with the market below 2012, you might place your buy stop (to get out of the short position) above that price. But in addition to exiting the short position, you could use a stop reversal to initiate a long position at that price.

Exercise 3.4

1. The most prominent feature is that the 200-day moving average does not follow the pattern of the price line. Because of its duration, the 200-day moving average is far smoother than a chart of the real-time prices. However, looking at the 200-day moving average on the chart you can see that it is curving downward while the market price line also is trending downward despite gyrations up and down.

2. When the market is trending downward (September 2000 to October 2000) it is above the 200-day moving average. As that distance narrows, however, the market found support at that level, as evidenced by the market activity roughly on that moving average line. As downward pressure increased, the market broke below the 200-day moving average, which accelerated the down move. Finding support, the market traded up to the moving average line in early November 2000, but could not break above it, which added to the negative pressure on the market.

3. The most prominent feature is that the 20-day moving average more closely follows the pattern of the price line until roughly January 2001, but then lags the uptrend until the lines cross in mid-February 2001. Because it has a shorter duration, the 20-day moving average has more peaks and valleys than the smoother 200-day moving average.

4. *False.* Granted, you may be watching shorter-term moving averages for trading signals, but it's also important to note—as far as overall market dynamics are concerned—where key moving averages such as the 200-day come into play. For example, on

April 16, 2001, Microsoft closed above its 200-day moving average, a significant move given the pressure that this stock and other technology issues had been under. Further, that event was significant to both the long-term and short-term players in Microsoft and the Nasdaq.

5. *False.* One of our technicians at TeachTrade.com uses 20 moving averages (10 on each screen) to analyze certain key markets. Realistically, you may not choose to use that many. But over time, you may find that certain moving averages work best to identify key points in the market. Therefore, you may use several to help you track the short-, intermediate-, and long-term dynamics of the market.

6. *True.* To find the best moving averages for your trading parameters, you will study several of them. In each case, look for the correlation between the line and the market, especially where the market generates buy and sell signals.

Exercise 3.5

1. The purpose of a trend line is to project the path if a trend continued into the future. The trend line then becomes a reference point (support and/or resistance) for real-time prices.

2. *True.* A trend line that connects three highs or lows is more important than one that connects only two. Having three or more highs/lows on the line validates its significance as a resistance/support line.

3. B. A rangebound market is *a market in which there are no significant new highs and no significant new lows.* It's as if the highs act as a ceiling and the lows make a floor, and the market simply moves from one barrier to the other. Sometimes we refer to this market as consolidating, particularly after a major move to the upside or downside.

4. B. *Contraction.* The most accurate answer is that the market is contracting, getting into a tighter and tighter range and setting up for the next move.

5. A. *Breakout.* In a contraction, the market is setting up for a breakout. Think of the contraction as the coiling of a spring, tighter and tighter. At some point, that spring is going to be released. Similarly, when the market contracts, it's gathering energy in the form of pent-up selling or buying interest for a breakout in one direction or the other.

4

Answers to Technical Analysis 102

Exercise 4.1

1. An uptrend is defined by higher highs and higher lows. The market is moving upward because there are more buyers than sellers. In terms of market activity, the abundance of buyers in the market means that sellers are able to get increasingly higher prices for what they supply. Buyers, meanwhile, have to "pay up" for whatever they want because of the higher demand.

2. A downtrend is defined by lower highs and lower lows. The market is moving downward because there are more sellers than buyers. In terms of market activity, the abundance of sellers means that buyers are able to pay lower prices for what they want because of the increase in supply. Sellers, meanwhile, have to lower their prices because of the decreasing demand.

3. The change in a trend is called a reversal. This may be price-driven, or it may be event-driven (and therefore the price is affected). For example, there may be heavy selling in a stock until either the supply at that price is exhausted or buyers step in

again because they think the stock is cheap at this level. Conversely, there may be heavy buying in a stock until the demand is exhausted, or sellers step in again because they think the stock is too expensive at this level. When these moves are triggered by an event or a surprise announcement—earnings-related news on a stock—these moves tend to be emotional, which may lead to overbuying and overselling.

Exercise 4.2

1. The chart of Veritas Software (VRTS) in the example shows a V bottom, with a low below $40 a share in late March 2001. While the formation is hardly a perfect V, the general shape is clear on the chart. It is interesting to note that the move downward took more time than the move upward, and once the upward trend was established the stock price continued to rise.

2. A chart may show one dramatic pattern—as in the case of the V in the Veritas chart—as well as smaller patterns. This is similar to looking at a mosaic. At first you see the big picture. Then you may see the smaller pictures or tiles that make up the entire scene or portrait. In this example, you can see smaller U patterns formed, such as from April 20 through May 1.

Exercise 4.3

1. In this M formation, the first high is above $45 a share, while the second high (the second peak of the M) is below $45. This is a classic failed retest of the highs.

2. After the second peak, the market sold off sharply, which is also indicative of a failed retest of the highs.

3. The M pattern indicates a failed retest of the highs. In this case, BEA Software traded above $45 a share, but could not exceed that level on the second try. Based on this pattern, you would as-

sume that the $45 price level would be strong resistance on sub-
sequent price moves. In fact BEAS failed to trade over $45 for
the remainder of May 2001.

Exercise 4.4

1. B. *Fake-out.* A market that appears to be breaking out to the upside but cannot sustain a rally or that appears to be breaking to
   the downside but cannot sustain the downside momentum is
   called a fake-out.

2. B. *Sometimes.* There are times when it's fairly easy to determine
   that there is a strong likelihood of a rally or breakout being sustained, such as when the market has just ended a time of contraction, with a tightening range that will send the market
   eventually in one direction or another, often with good velocity.
   In addition, if the market breaks out to the upside or breaks to
   the downside with strong volume, it has a good chance of being
   sustained. However, there are times when the market appears to
   be making a significant move but there is no follow-through at
   the new higher or lower levels.

3. *True.* There are times when the market is more apt to make a false
   breakout, particularly when the market is emotionally charged. For
   example, after interest rate action (a cut or a hike) is announced by
   the Federal Reserve, it's not uncommon to see three fake-outs before the market determines its final direction. What's happening in
   those fake-outs is that the market is reacting emotionally to the
   news. In early 2001 rate cuts often resulted in spikes in the stock
   index futures markets (as well in the prices of some individual equities), but the moves were not sustainable. Then the market would
   sell off nearly as sharply as it climbed, only to have it reverse
   sharply as the emotional tide turned once more.

4. *True.* Unfortunately, the only certain way to tell if a move is a
   breakout or a fake-out is after the fact. However, as stated in the
   preceeding answer, there are times when fake-outs are more

likely because of the nature of market conditions and/or because of an emotionally charged announcement such as Fed action. For example, knowing that fake-outs are common after the Fed makes such announcements can help traders to protect themselves from these fake-outs. In this scenario, you might expect the market to have a fake-out to the upside after a Fed announcement. Depending on your trading plan and market analysis, you might decide to buy after the up move was established, but you would look to sell fairly quickly, anticipating that the upward momentum might not be sustained.

Exercise 4.5

1. Trend lines can be drawn between any two highs or lows. For this exercise, draw a line from the highest point on the chart (mid-September, when the stock is over $45 a share) to the next significant high (late September/early October) at $41–$42 a share). Extending that line, you delineate resistance that caps this market all the way through mid-December, when it finally crosses that line and breaks out to the upside. Connecting the low at roughly $23 a share to the low at about $26 a share yields a support line that acts as a floor for this market until it is breached to the downside in early February 2001.

2. Interestingly, the point at which this market breaks that support line is also confirmed by the 50-day moving average line, which the market also breaches at about the same point. Also, the 200-day moving average contains much of the market's moves.

3. Looking at the chart, you can see a V at the low around $23 a share, as well as the rough price symmetry made on that move from about $37 a share in October to near $35 a share in late January.

4. Watching the market's behavior as it trades at or near key price levels—moving average lines and/or support and resistance levels—can help you to determine your trading strategy, real-time.

Exercise 4.6

1. A moving average is a line that depicts the average of prices for a specific period of time. For example, the 10-day moving average line depicts the average of prices over the previous 10 days. The shorter the time frame, the more reactive the moving average tends to be.

2. Trend lines are linear representations of prevailing trends. These trends may be plotted on any chart, depending on the time frame. You may chart a longer-term trend on a 6- or 12-month chart (or longer) or the short-term trends on a daily or intraday chart.

3. Moving average envelopes are one way to determine the limits or expected range of the market, given previous trade activity. For example, you may find that a 5 percent moving average envelope contains the highs and lows made for a specific time frame. Thus, that envelope would likely mark the expected resistance and support for the market going forward.

4. Similarly, trend channels also delineate the expected support and resistance areas within a prevailing trend.

5. Utilizing more than one indicator is useful in obtaining a consensus of opinion among your indicators to help you find and confirm your trading signals.

5

Answers to The Myths, the Risks, and the Rewards

Exercise 5.1

1. *False.* Your risk/reward ratio should ideally be 1:2 or better. In other words, what you stand to make on a trade should be at least twice as much as you stand to lose. This will govern your entry and exit points, as well as your stop placement.

2. *True.* The best way to limit your losses is with the strict use of stops. Even if you are stopped out on a trade and then the market proceeds to move exactly as you anticipated it would, congratulate yourself on your discipline to use a stop and stick with it.

3. *False.* There is one instance in which a stop can be moved during a trade, and that is when you are using a trailing stop, which moves in the direction of the market. But *never widen* a stop during a trade because you believe the market will turn around and wipe out your loss. That only increases your risk and the potential loss you will face if the market goes increasingly against you.

4. *False.* If you have had a string of losing trades, you should *cut down* your trading size. Losses can undermine your confidence

and your discipline. If you trade small, that ideal trade setup will increase your chance of making a profitable trade (albeit on a smaller scale) and decrease your risk exposure. After losses, the most important thing is to recover your confidence and your discipline—not necessarily to make up for previous losses.

5. Absolutely *true*. As a trader, your focus must be on limiting your risk and therefore preserving your capital. This can be summed up in two bits of trading wisdom:

   • Preserve your capital to come back and trade another day.

   • Never shoot your whole wad on any single trade.

Exercise 5.2

1. With a strict 2:1 ratio of reward to risk (or 1:2 risk to reward, if you prefer!) your protective sell stop would be placed at $18.625. However, your technical analysis may indicate a key price level at, say, $18.75, which would adjust your stop placement.

2. In this scenario, you would place your exit target (buying contracts to cover your short position) just above the support zone of 1299–1300. To do this, you might enter a buy order—MIT (market-if-touched) at 1300 or 1300.50 if you anticipate that buyers might step in at or before the support zone.

3. Keeping a 2:1 reward-to-risk ratio, you'd place a protective buy stop no higher than 1307.50, which corresponds with the resistance area at 1306–1307.

Exercise 5.3

1. In this scenario, to keep your reward-to-risk ratio at 2:1 or better, you would place your protective buy stop no higher than 1312. Since your technical analysis has pinpointed resistance at 1311,

you may want to put your protective buy stop in just over that level, for example, at 1311.20 or 1311.40.

2. If you scale out of your short position, you would likely use a trailing stop, which would move in the direction of the trade. In this case, if you continued to be short half a position below 1305.20 with a secondary target above 1300, you would likely move your protective stop to or below the 1305.20. That way if the market turned around suddenly, you would exit the second half of the position at or near the first exit price.

Exercise 5.4

1. *False.* Theoretically, your technical analysis should be as valid for 10 contracts as it is for one contract, or for 1,000 shares as it is for 100 shares. Placing the larger trade is as easy as well. However, there are two big considerations that potentially can make a difference when you increase your trade size. One is slippage. Typically, the larger you trade, the more slippage—the difference between the price you see on your screen and the price at which your market order is executed—becomes a factor. In addition, the increased capital exposure may be a detriment to your trading discipline. In other words, if you find it too stressful to increase your trading size, then don't. Remember, the most important part of trading is to know yourself, including your strengths and weaknesses.

2. *True.* It is important to disassociate yourself from the money on the line by focusing first on making a well-executed trade. However, you cannot forget about the money to the point that you lose respect for it.

3. *True.* To be successful you must be able to trade in virtually every kind of market (rangebound, trending, breakout, etc.). Being able to trade with a variety of strategies—and including from either the short or the long side—will help you to increase your potential of being and staying profitable.

4. *False.* Your goal is to trade the size that's right for you, your risk tolerance, your capitalization, and the market conditions.

5. *False.* When you trade, you must keep in mind that having a stop is no guarantee that you will get out at that price. In a fast-moving market your actual fill may be far above or below (depending on the market's direction) your stop target. For example, if you have a protective buy stop at 1305, but S&P futures sky-rocket suddenly, there is no guarantee that your stop will be filled at 1305. It could be 1305.50 or 1306. If you are trading a particularly volatile market or stock, you must take this into account when you are determining your stop placement.

Exercise 5.5

1. *False.* Daily trading profit goals can put your focus on the results of each trade, each day—instead of on making well-executed trades, win or lose. It's far better to have a well-executed losing trade (with your losses cut short at a predetermined stop) than to have a poorly executed winning trade that teaches and reinforces bad habits. Daily profit targets can make traders too desperate to make up for daily losses or to make something happen when the market conditions don't warrant it.

2. *False.* A very big danger—but a very common mistake—is wrapped up in the thinking of "if I make $500 a day, then I'll make $2,500 a week and then $125,000 a year—even with two weeks of vacation." This is an unrealistic goal. You will have losing days, and if you then expect to make up for each loss the next day, you run the risk of trading too actively or too frequently for the market conditions. Or you may trade too big for your experience level or your capitalization in hopes of making up for previous losses.

3. *True.* A far better discipline is to have longer-term profit goals that are realistic and attainable. In fact, you may want to have more than one set of goals. You may want to have a profit target

for each week or month of typical trading, and when market conditions are ideal for your style of trading (good volume, a strong trend that you can identify and trade, etc.) you may want to have a higher profit target for that week or month.

4. *False.* If you think you can trade for only a few hours a day and then have free time for the remainder of the day, you will seriously undermine your success and your profit potential. Trading is a full-time profession. Even if you actively trade only a few hours a day, the rest of the time must be spent with technical analysis, studying the market, reading and studying about trading, and analyzing your own trades. If you become successful at trading, it is likely to become a full-time profession/obsession.

5. *True.* Having a maximum loss each day will help you to develop a discipline that tells you when to quit for the day. When your losses amount to a certain level, it's imperative that you stop trading. You may want to paper trade, observe the market, dissect what you've done wrong, or get away from the market to clear your head. But if you continue to trade, you will increase the likelihood that your losses will get bigger.

Exercise 5.6

1. *False.* Beginning traders may favor one style of trading—playing the breakouts or buying the dips/selling the rallies. But successful traders know how to trade virtually any kind of market conditions, from both the short and the long side.

2. *True.* As discussed in the preceeding answer, to increase your effectiveness in the market and therefore your chances of success, you must learn and become competent at more than one trading strategy.

3. *True.* Just as it's important to recognize the trade setup and execute, you must also know when it's better to wait on the sidelines. For example, if the market is in a neutral or transition zone

and does not have a clear direction, this is not an optimal time to place a trade. In these circumstances, it would be better to wait for a trade setup to materialize.

4. *True.* Never try to pick tops and bottoms. If you do, more often than not your execution will be a compromise. Watch for the trade signal that tells you, for example, that the market will meet resistance that will put a top on the current move. Then wait for the confirmation from the marketplace. When you see that happening, it's time to sell—but not before the confirmation.

5. *False.* The trend is your friend. But if you get on the trend too late, then it won't do you any good. For example, if the market rallies but you wait too long before initiating a long position, you run the potential risk of buying at or near the top. That's why the timing is just as important as the trend itself.

6. *False.* Overtrading is not only real, it's a real potential danger for all traders. In overtrading, you trade too frequently and/or too large for the market conditions. One of the times when you may be susceptible to overtrading is when you have experienced a loss that shook your confidence or that you're trying to make up for quickly.

7. *False.* Adding to a losing position is just that—a losing position that is potentially getting bigger. There are times when you want to buy in at a variety of prices or sell at a variety of prices because to scale in or out is part of your strategy and in line with your technical analysis. This is a far cry, however, from adding to a losing position in hopes that the market will turn around and make up for all your previous losses. For example, if you go long a stock at, say, $20 a share, and then it declines sharply, it's far better to get out at a predetermined loss level and wait for the next setup. But if you then decide to buy more at $19.25, then $19, then $18.50, then $18, and then $17.50 . . . just because each time you think (hope, wish, and pray) that it's found a bottom, then you're guilty of adding to a losing position. Occasionally the market will eventually find a bottom and then rally, and you may get bailed out. But the risk is far greater that the market

will keep going against you until you have too large a position, a poor risk/reward ratio, and no sound technical analysis behind your trades.

Exercise 5.7

1. *True.* In the beginning, the "ready, aim, fire" process may feel very deliberate. But the goal is to teach yourself to look for setups, recognize setups, and then execute based on those setups.

2. *False.* Even after 20 years of trading, I still have a "ready, aim, fire" process for my trade. Granted, when I'm trading in the pit, that three-step process may look like a blur. But if I break down the steps of my trades, I will still find a three-step process of looking for the setup, finding and confirming the setup, and executing the trade.

3. *False.* During your learning curve, you may miss out on some quick moves. But it's far better to execute slowly and deliberately on the setups that you recognize and can confirm. Proficiency in trading is a skill that is gained with experience and over time.

6

Answers to Intraday Dynamics

Exercise 6.1

1. *True.* The Chicago Mercantile Exchange describes fair value as an "arbitrage free" level at which futures theoretically should be priced in relation to the cash index values, in the absence of transaction costs. Fair value typically reflects the cash or "spot" index value (such as the S&P 500 cash or SPX), plus financing charges (reflecting current prevailing interest rates), less any dividends that would accrue and be paid on the stocks in the underlying index.

2. *False.* Fair value does not change intraday. Rather, a futures contract may trade at a premium or a discount to what the fair value is on a particular day.

3. *True.* When futures trade at a significant discount or premium to fair value, it sets up an arbitrage opportunity for large players in the market. Typically, program trading is triggered, in which futures are sold and stocks are bought, or vice versa, until the market comes back into line with fair value.

133

Exercise 6.2

1. You have already identified 1306–1307 as resistance for the market. The opening range of 1305–1307 actually contained that resistance area. After the market tried unsuccessfully to break out above the range (but was unable to sustain trading above 1308) and then couldn't recover when it returned to the opening range, a downward bias has been confirmed. With the market now below the opening range, the resistance area at 1306 all the way up to 1308 has been established and confirmed as intraday resistance.

2. With support confirmed at 1299–1300 and buyers stepping in above this level, you would likely look to establish a long position above 1300.

3. Your initial profit target would likely be about 50 percent of the daily range thus far. With a high at 1308 and a low at 1299, the midway point would be at 1303.50, at which you would likely sell out at least half of your long position. If buying momentum remained strong, you might opt to scale out of half of your position at 1303.50 and carry the rest toward the resistance area at 1306 to 1308. You may also opt (depending on the buying activity that you observe) to scale out of the remainder starting at 1305.

4. Nothing. At 1303.50, the market is between support at 1299.50 and resistance that begins at 1306 and extends up to the high at 1308. This is known as a "50/50" trade, meaning that from 1303.50 the market could go either way: down to 1299.50 support or up to the 1306–1308 resistance cluster.

5. If the market traded up to and through 1308, it has shown significant upside strength to break through the resistance cluster to the upside. At this point, you'd be looking for confirmation of a continuing uptrend (such as dominance from the buyers, or a trend line that indicates support above 1308). If that occurs, with a short-term day-trading perspective you would be looking to go long above 1308 for the next profit target. The opening range would then become support.

Exercise 6.3

1. Significant price levels that you would look for as part of your technical analysis include: previous highs and lows, previous settlement prices, and the prices at which certain trend lines (resistance or support) come into play.

2. These price levels would act as reference points for your trading strategy. If, for example, the market is above the previous day's close, you would look for confirmation of an uptrend. If there is a previous high above the market, that level would likely be resistance, while a previous low below the market would be support. The market, however, tends to challenge those previous highs and lows to see if they can be broken. You would watch closely how the market acted at and around those price levels. If one of those price levels were breached, you'd be watching for follow-through buying or selling in the direction of the trend, to determine if the move is good or just a fake-out.

Exercise 6.4

1. *True.* Retracements are price points that equate to specific percentages of a previous major move. These percentages include 25 percent, 33 percent, 50 percent, 75 percent, 88 percent, as well as 38.2 percent and 61.8 percent. For example, in the TeachTrade.com Morning Meeting commentary on May 31, 2001, we noted that in the Nasdaq futures market the price level of 1718 was a 50 percent retracement of the recent up move from 1360 to 2076. Because of that, 1718 became a target for traders to watch.

2. *False.* Retracements can be plotted along any significant move in the market, including rallies or breaks.

3. *True.* In the case of retracements, market psychology does play a large role. For example, in the first answer, because 1718 is a 50 percent retracement of a recent major move, one could easily

expect that price to be on the radar screen of many traders. For that reason alone, it would become a target when the market approached that level.

4. Based on our experience, 88 percent retracements tend to mark the end of a significant move. Thus, with the market at $35.75, you would begin to exit the last portion of your trade around $36 to $36.25. Perhaps the upward momentum would extend beyond $36.25. But the risk would increase significantly that sellers would step in at or before that $36.25 level.

Exercise 6.5

1. In this scenario, S&Ps gapped lower, and the gap was not filled on that day. Therefore, you would expect S&Ps to finish lower (the direction of the gap) on the day. In fact, S&Ps did close that day 53 points lower than the previous day.

2. There's a saying, "Nature abhors a vacuum." In the case of the market, if there is a gap within reach, the market typically tries to fill it. In this scenario, with the market under pressure, you would expect this leftover gap to act as a target.

Exercise 6.6

1. If a candlestick chart shows progressively higher closes with a formation that resembles steps in a staircase, that is a classic example of an uptrend.

2. A "doji" is formed when the open and close of a particular bar (such as one representing 30 minutes on a 30-minute chart) are at the same price. This kind of activity often signals a trend reversal.

3. If the market needs to get above a particular price for an uptrend to remain intact, with an hourly close above this level the uptrend has been strengthened and the market's bias is bullish.

4. If the market closed below a certain level on an hourly basis, the bias becomes bearish and the level would become resistance on any retest of that level.

Exercise 6.7

1. An M is formed intraday when the market sells off from a recent high (this may be the daily high or an intraday high) and then attempts to retest that level. The significance would be to confirm resistance, intraday, at that level of the failed retest of the high.

2. If a V is formed touching a 10-minute moving average, this would confirm support at this level. The market has support at the bottom of the V, which coincides with a bounce off the moving average.

3. After a stock gapped at the open and moved higher and a W—a failed retest of the lows—formed above the gap, these two factors—the gap open and the W—signal and confirm a bullish trend.

Exercise 6.8

1. *True.* Limits are designed to enforce a pause in market activity to slow a dramatic move in the market.

2. *True.* Price limits must become part of your strategy for two major reasons: In the case of S&P or Nasdaq futures, for example, trading is temporarily suspended at limit down. Further, as the market approaches limits, they tend to act as magnets. Thus if Nasdaq is at 1930 and limit down is at 1925, the market will tend to trade toward the limit level.

3. Once a futures contract is locked limit down, you must focus on the corresponding cash market. It is critical for a trader to know exactly where the cash was trading when the limit was hit in the futures contract. So, while you are unable to trade

the futures, you can see the fluctuations in the underlying cash market. You can discern from the activity in the cash market whether the limit in the futures was caused by widespread selling or by just a single seller in the futures who moved the market lower, meaning it will likely bounce back after the limit expires.

4. Here's one scenario for trading after a limit-down move: Let's say a futures contract is not traded for the full 10-minute limit time. When it reopens for trading, the market is below the limit. Traders often expect the market, at some point, to bounce back to the limit price. Therefore, it's not uncommon to see buying after the market has locked limit down and opens lower in anticipation of a bounce back to the previous limit.

Exercise 6.9

1. The 1920 level is established and confirmed as resistance. Since the market opened well below that level, struggled to reach 1920, and was unable to break through it to the upside, this adds to the downward pressure on the market at or near 1920.

2. If a reversal does develop in the preceeding scenario, the two key prices to watch initially would be the 1920-high area and the opening level of 1913.

3. To fade this move, you would look to be a buyer over 1913 and sell as the market is reaching the 1920 high.

4. If the market retests old highs/lows but fails to penetrate these levels, they are confirmed as resistance and support. Thus, if the market is contained by these two extremes—old highs and old lows—one way to fade trade would be to sell just as the market is reaching the area of the old highs and buy just as the market is reaching the old lows.

Exercise 6.10

1. *False.* The market trend and/or bias can change intraday for a variety of reasons. Perhaps an unexpected news announcement brings buyers (bullish sentiment) or sellers (bearish sentiment) into the market. Or an individual stock or a stock index may be able to breach resistance or support, which in turn creates follow-through buying or selling that can change the trend.

2. *True.* A short-term trend and a long-term trend can be opposing. Think back to the charts you studied in Chapters 3 and 4 of this workbook. The overall pattern may have been an uptrend or a downtrend. But within that overall pattern, there are many "mini patterns"—gyrations up and down that reflect short-term trends. Put another way, a stock may decline in price over a two-month period from, say, $75 a share to $52 a share. But within those two months it could close higher on several days.

3. *True.* Here is one of the simplest examples of how two traders can make money: Trader #1 is short a stock from $75 to $50. At $50 he covers his short position profitably. Another trader could have a bullish bias at $50 and go long at that price for an anticipated retracement of the $75-to-$50 down move. Another example: A futures day trader could be long S&Ps from 1300 and sell out at 1304; a futures trader with a longer-term horizon may have a trend line come in at 1304, at which she buys for an eventual run (over the course of several days) to 1315.

4. *True.* Unfortunately, you may be right about a trend but still have a losing trade. Why? The timing of your trade could be too premature for the trend to develop fully in the marketplace. For example, your trading analysis may have generated a buy signal. But outside factors—a surprise news announcement, selling in a related stock or index—could pressure the stock or market that

you're trading. After you've been stopped out with a loss, you could very well see a recovery in the stock or market you were trading. But you still had a losing trade. Your analysis was right, but the timing was wrong. That's why you must always control your risk and protect your capital on every trade, regardless of how sure you are of a trend.

7

Answers to Trading the Nasdaq

Exercise 7.1

1. *True.* Nasdaq is a very volatile index, reflecting the gyrations of the component stocks that dominate it. Nasdaq futures, for example, have about three times greater volatility than S&P futures.

2. C. The Nasdaq Composite ended 1999 with an *85.6 percent* gain over the previous year.

3. A. At the end of 2000, the Nasdaq Composite was off *39.3 percent.*

4. In a nutshell, the so-called "tech wreck" that is being blamed for the Nasdaq decline was reflective of inflated price/earnings (P/E) ratios for technology stocks that skyrocketed in 1999 and then collapsed in 2000 when reality set in. The promise of the Internet and e-commerce did pale somewhat, but it would be incorrect to say that the Internet is no longer viable as a business tool.

5. From a psychological perspective the "spike up/spike down" pattern has resulted in a lot of nervous investors who were disillusioned or potentially burned financially by the gyrations in this

market. Technically speaking, when a market goes through that kind of "spike up/spike down," it is not uncommon to see a lot of false starts afterward. In other words, it would not surprise us to see the Nasdaq repeatedly gain ground and then lose ground for a while as it tries to get a footing to move forward.

Exercise 7.2

1. Negative news after hours on a major stock in the Nasdaq 100 would most likely have a bearish impact on the index overall.

2. A positive news surprise in a major stock would be bullish for the Nasdaq 100. For example, after the close of the market on April 17, 2001, Intel announced quarterly net income that exceeded expectations and also made positive comments about the second half of the year. The next morning, Nasdaq futures—which had closed at 1672.50 on April 17—opened at 1775.

Exercise 7.3

1. The SOX is the Semiconductors index. If it is up—in this case 2.2 percent—it may reflect strength in the Nasdaq, or it made bode well for selling pressure in the Nasdaq to ease. Why? As a technology-dominated index, Nasdaq has many semiconductor stocks, and thus strength in the SOX would be a positive in general for Nasdaq. For individual stocks, you might see strength in one particular semiconductor stock that is also a positive sign for other semiconductor issues, or for technology issues in general. This "lay of the land" perspective is helpful for trading both indexes and individual issues.

2. With the SOX roughly unchanged and negative news affecting one of the big five, the Nasdaq may be more reflective of what's happening in the smaller issues. This would be a good time to watch

the second-tier stocks—those with market weightings just under the big five—for hints as to the near-term direction of the Nasdaq.

3. *False.* Even though IBM trades on the New York Stock Exchange, it is a technology stock and therefore could potentially impact the Nasdaq. For example, if news on IBM has ramifications for the technology sector, look for a ripple to go through the Nasdaq.

4. This would have a potentially strong bullish impact on the Nasdaq. In fact, this example is taken right out of recent history. On April 16, 2001, Microsoft closed above its 200-day moving average, which was a significant move, given the pressure that this stock and other technology issues had been under. In addition, what this move in Microsoft told us was that the biggest stock in the Nasdaq 100 had crossed a milestone, and because of this it gave us a hint that the rest of the index could be poised for at least a short-term turnaround.

Exercise 7.4

1. If your stops prove to be too narrowly placed for the current market volatility, you should consider widening your stops. One way to examine stop placement would be to plot the market's movement against a moving average envelope to help you see the swings intraday and where your stops should be placed.

2. Widening your stops will increase your overall risk. Basically, by widening your stops you are widening the parameters for a potentially unprofitable trade. Put another way, you are allowing the market to move farther against you before you exit the trade.

3. To compensate for these wider stops, you would have to cut down your trade size in order to keep your overall risk level in balance. With wider stops but trading a smaller position (less capital involved in a trade) you have kept your risk level in balance.

Exercise 7.5

1. That kind of rapid move with little activity along the way is known as an "air ball." This quick drop/quick rise phenomenon can occur in almost any market, but it is more likely to occur in a volatile market like the Nasdaq, in which volume may also be thinner than in other indexes.

Exercise 7.6

1. If the Nasdaq is extended at a very wide percentage (compared with recent activity) from the 20-day moving average, the odds at that point are slim that you'd get much more out of a long position.

2. A 6 percent extension is still within the recent normal extension limits for the Nasdaq. While you probably wouldn't trade based on this extension alone, if other factors contributed to the bearish sentiment a 6 percent extension from the moving average would not be enough to reverse that opinion.

3. While you may decide to exit your long position, you probably wouldn't jump into the market on the short side immediately. For one thing, there is still a chance that the market could extend further to the upside—although the odds of a continued significant move are slim. Rather, you'd wait and look for the market to reverse the next day or the day after that, to take advantage of the extended conditions.

Exercise 7.7

1. Nasdaq futures had traded lower overnight and now, at the start of the day's trading session, had gapped lower to 1900.50. The tone was definitely bearish. Moreover, the opening was right between two key zones: support between 1890 and 1885 and resistance between 1900 and 1910.

2. With a gap-lower opening and the sell-off on the overnight session, the tone was definitely bearish.

3. Lower highs and higher lows create a wedge or triangle pattern that typically signals a breakout.

4. Typically about three-quarters of the way through a triangle pattern a breakout would occur. The question would be in what direction?